NOBSKA

BEN CARNEVALE

PAGE PUBLISHING, INC.
Conneaut Lake, PA

First originally published by Page Publishing 2021

ISBN 978-1-6624-2576-9 (pbk)
ISBN 978-1-6624-2577-6 (digital)

Printed in the United States of America

CONTENTS

Chapter 7

Chapter 8

Chapter 10

PREFACE

BORN IN NEWTON, Massachusetts, in 1933, I was always fascinated by lighthouses along the Massachusetts coastlines. Everyone loves lighthouses, especially those who rely on their powerful beam or foghorn blasts for guidance and survival in troubled waters. People worldwide love to visit and learn about lighthouses. Some inquire about overnight or a few days' stay while others inquire about renting or even purchasing a lighthouse!

Nobska Light greets an average of 1,500 visitors each year, and it's interesting to hear the variety of questions asked, "When was the light tower painted white?" "Explain refraction," and "What's the difference between nautical and statute miles?"

As a ham radio operator with call sign W1VZT, I was privileged to have been assigned to set up and operate the club's radio station at Nobska Light several years ago during "Lighthouse Week." The purpose of this annual event was to offer ham radio operators an opportunity to make radio contact to as many "lighthouses" as possible worldwide. Awards are available, or a simple exchange of cards (QSL cards) to confirm contacts.

I am also privileged and honored to work with and learn from my tour guide colleagues. We want to make sure our visitors leave Nobska Light with knowledge of its history, as well as memories of its incredible views, equally as important, leave Nobska with all their questions answered. However, I occasionally found myself citing inaccurate historical information. The internet often contradicts and provides inaccurate data.

In fact, one source claimed some lighthouses can be seen far beyond the curvature of the earth despite giving focal planes of the light source! Another claimed ten oil lamps were used inside a Fresnel fifth-order lens—hardly enough space!

Yet another explained the many gallons of oil carried up many stairs daily to the lightroom without realizing the lens used only one oil lamp that burned less than a gallon a night! These discrepancies were obvious, but how about those not so obvious such as dates, focal plane, or keepers' names, for example?

Nobska visitors look for answers, and this book is intended to serve that purpose. Updated editions will be available as my Nobska research continues. Inaccuracies will be addressed, and new findings will be included. Please feel free to contact me should you detect any errors or if you simply wish to discuss any topic regarding Nobska (e-mail: Cricket7388@gmail.com).

Enjoy!

--- ⚓ ---

INTRODUCTION

WHEN WE TALK or write about the history of anything, our major areas of concern must be *details* and *accuracies*, right? Well, in my attempt to achieve such concerns, I visited many institutions over the last several years to locate original Nobska documents and feel I have provided Nobska Lighthouse enthusiasts with a book that consolidates Nobska's history and reference data into one convenient source—between two covers!

This book is intended to be read from cover to cover or scanned through the "contents" to immediately find areas of interest or concern, to review what you already know, or learn about some historical information you may not have known. Chapters 1 through 5 covers from the 1829 original Nobska Light to the 1876 rebuilding of Nobska Light, to the keepers of Nobska Light, to the fog-signaling equipment. The glossary in the back will explain unfamiliar lighthouse terms. You will find "Nobska Time Line at a Glance" toward the back of the book very handy.

Chapter 9 explains how far a light can be seen from various heights above sea level using simple formulas and also explains how nautical miles came to be, and chapter 10 explains the science of finding your longitude anywhere on the planet.

I love being a Nobska tour guide, I love interacting with our visitors, and above all, I love to share the history and breathtaking views from our beautiful *Nobska*!

Please enjoy the ride.

ACKNOWLEDGMENTS

THANK YOU TO everyone who graciously offered their help and assistance during my research for this book. I am forever grateful.

Dr. Don Abt *for his valuable time and answers to my hard questions.*

Joanne Blum-Carnevale, my lovely and talented wife, *for her understanding, endless patience, lighthouse knowledge, proofreading, and valuable contributions to this book. (Joanne is also a Nobska tour guide.)*

Catherine Bumpus, director, Friends of Nobska Light, *for her warm welcome to access documents.*

Peter Collom, commander USCG, (retired), and Edna Collom, *for their warm welcome, their answers, and their stories.*

Chad Cortes, chief electrician's mate, USCG, *for his patience, valuable time, and answers.*

Meg Costillo, Falmouth Museums on the Green, *for her help and assistance.*

Jeremy D'Entremont, author, *for his valuable time, for answering difficult questions, and for his informative books and articles.*

David Skena, first class petty officer, USCG, *for his patience, valuable time, and answers.*

Thomas Tag, author, *for his valuable time, for answering difficult questions, and for his informative books and articles.*

Susan Wetzel, Woods Hole Historical Museum, *for her help and assistance.*

United States Lighthouse Society *for their outstanding articles and for which I am a proud member.*

CHAPTER 1

Original Nobska Light Station (1829)

In the Beginning

DURING THE MID to late 1700s, smallpox was a very serious disease in America, in fact, an epidemic. There had been a smallpox inoculation hospital in Falmouth Heights on Cape Cod, Massachusetts, in 1777, run by Dr. George Donaldson and a second hospital established at Nobska Point in Woods Hole, Falmouth, in 1797, run by Dr. Francis Wicks when the population in Woods Hole was only about ten houses. Nobska Point was selected for the second hospital site because of its remote location from other Falmouth villages.[1]

Vessel Traffic

During the late 1700s, many vessels passed by Nobska Point while traveling eastbound and westbound through Nantucket Sound, Vineyard Sound, and Buzzards Bay. This was a major route to and from Boston, New York, Philadelphia, Baltimore, and other major seaports with many vessels carrying lumber, coal, bricks, salt, fertil-

---

[1] *Book of Falmouth*, second edition 1988. Dr. George Hugh Donaldson (1755–1836) and Dr. Francis Wicks (1752–1812) traveled to England in 1797 to obtain vaccines for the two hospitals to treat patients living in Falmouth villages against the smallpox disease. Massachusetts was the first state in the United States to provide vaccinations for smallpox.

izer, and other goods. Whaling traffic was also very heavy through this passage as well.

Due to this heavy traffic, there was an overwhelming amount of shipwrecks, and therefore, a need for lighthouses. In 1789, the US government began to install a series of lighthouses along this route.

Spider Lamps

Lighthouse lightrooms were equipped with "spider" lamps, which consisted of a shallow brass pan filled with whale oil and several wicks hanging over the edges of the pan resembling a spider. Spider lamps were first used in the Boston Light and were known to produce dangerous fumes, which burned the eyes of keepers.

Spider lamps were not very effective as a source for light, and because of this, there was a need to brighten lighthouses in the United States.

The Need for Brighter Lights

Buy the Patent

In 1810, Winslow Lewis, a former New England ship captain, lighthouse builder, and resident of Wellfleet on Cape Cod, Massachusetts, patented a lighting system[2] for lighthouses consisting of an Argand-type oil lamp with a magnifying green glass lens in front of the lamp and a silver-plated parabolic reflector behind the lamp. On June 20 of the same year, Lewis offered to sell his patent to the US government, including installing his lamps in lighthouses throughout the United States.

The Argand oil lamp used in the Winslow Lewis patent was invented in 1782 by physicist and mathematician Aimè Argand of Geneva Switzerland while he was living in France. The Argand lamp used whale oil fed by gravity from a reservoir mounted above the base of a hollow circular-shaped wick. Hot air created by the flame increased

---

[2] Patent no. 1305.

and guided the flow of oxygen through and around the cylindrical wick. Argand also invented the chimney, which he specifically designed for his oil lamps. His chimney had a small opening on top to increase the flow of rising hot air. His design stabilized air currents, thus allowing the flame to burn brighter than conventional lamps without chimneys.

The Lewis lighting system, with its modified Argand lamp, provided a farther luminous range through poor visibility conditions than any other type of lamp in the United States.

After the government gave the approval to test the Lewis lamp at Boston Lighthouse, Lewis received a letter from the government recommending his lamps. Lewis then signed a contract with the government in 1812 to sell his patent for $25,000, which included installing his lamp systems in lighthouses throughout the United States within a two-year period, then maintain all the lamps for the next seven years.[3]

It's interesting to note from the Lewis list below that lighthouses during this period used as many as thirty-one oil lamps as in the Sandy Hook Light in New Jersey and as few as five oil lamps in the Squam Light in Gloucester, Massachusetts.

---

[3] The contract agreement between the government and Lewis stipulated that Lewis would install lens/lamp/reflector lighting systems in lighthouses throughout the United States. Although Nobska was provided with a ten-lamp system, other lighthouses were provided with anywhere from five to thirty-one, depending on location and purpose of the lighthouses.

Light Houses from the Chesapeake to Maine.

Names.	No. of lamps	Names.	
Cape Henry	14	New Port	10
Old Point Comfort	10	Goat Island	8
New Point Comfort	9	Clark's Point	8
Smiths Point	9	Bird Island	10
Bodkin	13	Cutter hunk	9
North Point	18	Gay Head	10
Cape Henlopen	13	Tarpauling cove	7
Cape May	15	West Chop	9
Fort Delaware	8	One lamp added by the	
Sandy Hook	31	Order of Mr. Claiborn	
Sands Point	11	Cape Poge	6
Eaton's Neck	12	Brand Point	
Old Field Point	10	Nantucket	13
Montauk Point	13	Point Gammon	7
Gull Island	14	Monamoy	
Black Rock	8	Chatham	14
New Haven	8	Cape Cod	16
Stratford Point	10	Race Point	10
Faulkner Island	12	Billingsgate	8
Lynde Point	7	Plymouth	12
New London	9	Situate	7
Stonington	10	Boston	14
Watch Hill	10	Long Island head	10
Point Judith	10	Baker's Island	24

Part 1 of 2: Lewis oil lamp quantities used at various lighthouses that Lewis agreed to maintain.

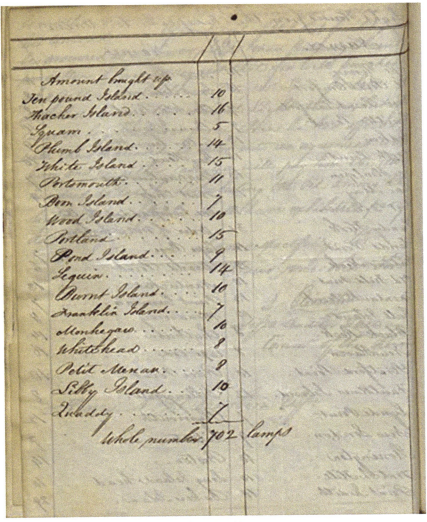

Amount brought up	
Ten pound Island	10
Thacher Island	16
Squam	5
Plumb Island	14
White Island	15
Portsmouth	11
Boon Island	7
Wood Island	10
Portland	15
Pond Island	9
Sequin	14
Burnt Island	10
Franklin Island	7
Monhegan	10
Whitehead	8
Petit Menan	9
Libby Island	10
Quaddy	7
Whole number	702 lamps

Part 2 of 2

The contract further stipulated that the Lewis lamp must be brighter and burn half the amount of oil burned by existing lamps. Although delays caused by the war of 1812, Lewis was able to successfully complete the installation by 1816.

Winslow Lewis
(1770 to July 1850)
(Photo courtesy United States Lighthouse Society [USLHS])

Aimè Argand
(July 5, 1750, to October 14, 1803)
(Photo courtesy United States Lighthouse Society [USLHS])

Building the Original Nobska Light

Buy the Land

Massachusetts ceded four acres of land on Nobska Point to the government in 1828 for the purpose of establishing a lighthouse station. On May 22 of the same year, Congress appropriated $3,000 to buy the land and to build a lighthouse station on Nobska Point. The government purchased the land on July 7, 1828, for $160. The smallpox inoculation hospital was taken down, and in 1829, the original Nobska Light Station was built for $2,949.30.

FORM 152.

General object (title of appropriations), and details and explanation.	Date of act making the appropriation.	Reference to the Statutes at Large. Volume.	Page.	Section.	Amount of annual appropriation.	Year of expenditure.	Expenditure by warrants.	Repayments.	Amount carried to the surplus fund.	Net expenditures.
Nobsque Point light-station. The act of May 22, 1828, provides, "That the Secretary of the Treasury be empowered to provide, by contract, for building a light-house on Nobsque Point, in the State of Massachusetts."	May 22, 1828	4	281	1-2	3,000 00	1829	2,949 30			2,949 30
Total					3,000 00	1830	2,949 30		50 70	2,949 30
									50 70	

Appropriations document
Form 152 dated May 22, 1828
(*National Archives, Washington, DC*)

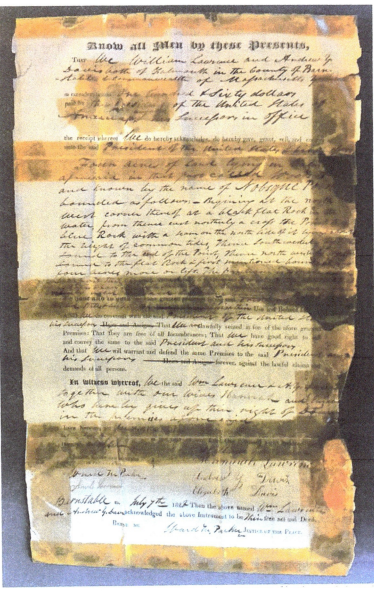

Government contract, dated July 7, 1828, to purchase four acres of land on Nobska Point from William and Hannah Lawrence and Andrew J. and Elizabeth Davis for $160 to construct a light station.
(National Archives, Washington, DC)

Construction

The keepers' dwelling at the Nobska Light Station was a one-and-a-half-story saltbox design made of stone and brick, approximately thirty-four feet by twenty feet. There were three rooms on the first floor and two rooms on the second floor. The first keeper to occupy this dwelling was Peter Daggett. An octagonal-shaped glass-enclosed lantern sixteen feet high by eight feet in diameter, referred to as the light tower, was attached to the center of the roof and housed the lighting system, which was provided and installed by Lewis.

Original Nobska Point Light Station built in 1829.
(Photo shows the 5th order lens, installed in 1856)

Lantern

The lantern employed horizontal astragal-framed glass panels and an outside wooden parapet (catwalk) with railing encircling the lightroom. The parapet was used by the keeper to observe weather conditions, marine traffic, marine activities, and to clear the windows from snow and ice accumulations. The height of the light produced an eighty-foot focal plane.[4]

Lightroom

The lightroom at Nobska included ten Lewis lighting assemblies. Each assembly consisted of a green glass magnifying lens/lamp/reflector. Four such assemblies were on an upper-tier hoop and six similar assemblies on a lower-tier hoop. This arrangement produced a fixed white light. The luminous range of this light system was approximately eight miles during clear evenings, less under poor visibility conditions.

Due to the long-term contractual agreement with Lewis, our government was not able to pursue the purchase and use of the newly designed and far superior Fresnel lenses, which were successfully being used by many other countries.

---

[4] Focal plane of a lighthouse light is the distance from the center of the outgoing horizontal light beam to the sea level at mean high water (MHW).

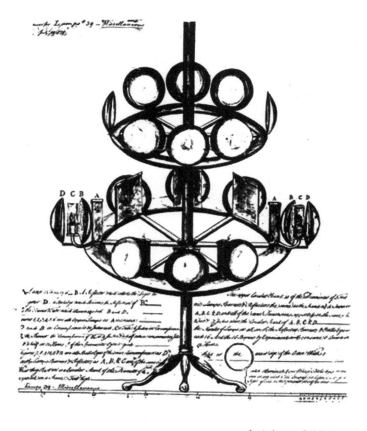

Winslow Lewis patent no. 1305 for a
green glass magnifying lens/lamp/reflector lighting system.
(Courtesy Thomas Tag and US Lighthouse Society [USLHS])

The lighting system was mounted on a pedestal, which was fastened to the center of the floor in the lightroom. The green glass magnifying lenses in front of the lamps were later removed by the government because they absorbed too much light, which diminished the luminous range.

Oil Consumption

The oil lamps were lit on an average of 15 hours during winter nights and 8 hours during summer nights, or 4,186 hours[5] annually. Although the lamps were lit at dusk and extinguished at dawn, the keeper kept the lamps lit during the day whenever poor visibility made it necessary to activate the fog bell.

Oil consumption was typically 339 gallons annually; 209 gallons during summer months, and 130 gallons during winter months.[6] The question as to why these lamps consumed *less* oil during long winter nights may be answered as follows: based on the ratio of 209 summer gallons, versus 130 winter gallons, the keepers' logbooks may have included spring and fall as *summer* months. The cost of oil during this period was $0.11 per gallon or $38.91[7] annually.

Maintenance

Costs to maintain the lightroom were very high. During every four-hour watch, the glass chimneys over the lamps had to be cleaned and dried of moisture, wicks trimmed, and lamps filled with oil then realigned for maximum brightness. Reflectors had to be polished then realigned for maximum brightness as well. Due to frequent polishing, the silver-plated fronts of the reflectors eventually wore off and would need to be replated or replaced.

The routine polishing of reflectors would often distort the relatively "thin" copper from which they were made. Reflectors would then need to be reshaped by the keeper to restore the maximum brightness of the lamp. All brass hardware associated with the lighting system had to be cleaned and polished as well. It was import-

---

5 At 182 winter nights per year × 15 night hours = 2,730 winter hours
   At 182 summer nights per year × 8 night hours = <u>1,456</u> summer hours
   <u>4,186</u> annual hours

6 Nobska Lighthouse keeper Peter Daggetts's 1845 logbook.
   National Archives, Washington, DC.
   Falmouth Museums on the Green Falmouth, Massachusetts.

7 *The Register*, April 21, 1983.

ant to carefully follow maintenance procedures provided by the US Lighthouse Establishment; otherwise, keepers could be removed from their duties.

Modifications to the Lantern

It appears that the lantern went through several height modifications possibly suggesting the need to increase the focal plane of the lighting system. In 1839, the height was increased to sixteen feet providing a focal plane of eighty feet, then ten years later, in 1849, the height was increased to twenty-four feet to provide an eighty-eight-foot focal plane.

Upgrade to a Fifth-Order Fresnel Lens

In 1856, a fifth-order Fresnel lens[8] and a single Argand-type oil lamp replaced the obsolete Lewis ten-lamp/reflector lighting system at the Nobska station. The new lens dramatically increased the luminous range at night, as well as during conditions of poor visibility. Fresnel lenses are very efficient. Only a small percentage of the source light is absorbed in its glass.

Although the initial cost for the Fresnel lens was high, the government realized the benefits and cost savings over a short period. This new lens produced a fixed white light, which was lit at dusk and extinguished at dawn. A cotton cover was placed over the lens for protection against sunrays during the day whenever the lamp was not lit.

---

[8] The focal distance, or focal length, of a lens is the dimension from its internal light source to inside the lens, or radius. This dimension, coupled with the brightness level of the light source, determines the power level, or order, of a lens. First order is most powerful; sixth order is least powerful. Refer to chapter 8 "Fresnel Lens."

Oil Consumption

Since the new fifth-order lens employed a single Argand oil lamp, oil consumption was dramatically reduced from 339 gallons per year to only 109 gallons per year—a 68 percent reduction of oil. The daily average oil consumption was 0.42 gallons per night. This reduction in oil usage became very important as the cost of oil in the 1850's significantly increased.

Cistern, Woodshed, and Barn

Although documentation has not been found on dates the cistern, woodshed, and barn were built, the keepers' logbook entries and inspection reports recorded that on November 10, 1862, "the woodshed roof was reshingled"; and in 1869, inspection report no. 87, "repairs of woodshed, barn…in progress."

88. Arlington Point. Corner boards of tower packed with point cement; walls of dwelling repointed; plastering repointed; cistern recemented; mixed studding in one room and reset base boards; sink built in kitchen; one window renewed, all others repaired and blinds repainted; new weather boards on east end of tower fitted; wooden edifices and one new trimmings repainted; two coats; new yard gate set; illuminating 1878

Inspection report no. 88: A cistern
was used in the original dwelling.
(National Archives, Washington, DC)

32

St. Kolsque Point.—Repairs of wood-shed, barn, and fences are now in progress. A shortien fireboard has been supplied and illuminating apparatus overhauled. 1869

Inspection report no. 87: Repairs were made
to the woodshed and barn in 1869.
(National Archives, Washington, DC)

Remove the Original Light Station

Over the next few decades, the roof of the Nobska Lighthouse had deteriorated and developed severe leaks due to the added weight[9] of the new fifth-order lens. In 1875, the lighthouse was taken down for fear that its roof would collapse.

Inspection report no. 114: Recommendation to rebuild the Nobska Light Station.
(*National Archives, Washington, DC*)

---

[9] It was reported that Robert J. Hindley, son of keeper Joseph G. Hindley, suggested there might have been a fire on the roof of the original lighthouse and thus contributing to its deterioration. However, documentation was not found by the author to support this claim.

---- ⚓ ----

CHAPTER 2

Rebuilt Nobska Light Station (1876)

Introduction

AFTER THE ORIGINAL lighthouse was taken down in 1876, a new Nobska Light Station was erected on Nobska Point. The light tower was "double-wall" constructed to facilitate the forty-foot tall and sturdy structure. The new light station included the light tower a separate keepers' dwelling, an oil house, and a woodshed. All structures were painted reddish brown. This color was chosen to allow the light tower to also serve as a day marker for mariners. The cost of the new Nobska Light Station was $50,000.[10]

Inspection report no. 115
(National Archives, Washington, DC)

---

[10]   National Register and the Massachusetts Historical Commission, 80 Boylston Street, Boston, Massachusetts, 02116, dated July 24, 1981, file 87001483.pdf.

Early photo of the Nobska Light Station rebuilt in 1876.

Rebuild the Nobska Light Station

Exterior Construction

The exterior shell was made from four individual cast-iron sections, each one-fourth-inch thick. The sections were manufactured in a foundry in Chelsea, Massachusetts, then transported by barge to the Woods Hole Harbor. The four sections were then moved by oxen to its present location on Nobska Point, Massachusetts, then assembled on site.

The bottom and largest first section was mounted to its solid cement foundation. The remaining sections were then fitted on top of one another. The four cast-iron sections were bolted together to form the traditional "conical" light tower configuration.

The outside diameter of the light tower at the base is fourteen feet six inches and ten feet six inches near the top. The fifth-order lens and oil lamp that was used in the original lighthouse was installed in the newly rebuilt lighthouse. The light tower was painted white for the *first* time in February 1913.[11]

Interior Construction

The interior wall of the light tower was brick-lined from the ground level to the watch room fourth level just below the light-room. The air space between the interior brick wall and the exterior cast-iron shell was intended to prevent condensation. Visitors have asked about the curvature of the interior wall, "Are the bricks curved?" The bricks are not curved. They are straight but laid to form the curvature pattern.

Lantern

Vent Ball

Hot air in the lightroom, generated by solar heat through the windows of the lantern, and from heat produced by the oil lamp, was exhausted through an external vent-ball fixture on the roof.

---

[11] Entry from keepers' logbook and *Barnstable Patriot* newspaper announcement, January 13, 1913. The light tower was painted white for the *first* time in February 1913.

Lightning arrester and vent ball fixture on the roof of the lantern.
(Photo by the author)

Lightning Arrester

A copper lightning arrester (rod), approximately three feet long, protrudes from the top of the vent ball in the center of the metal roof of the lantern. A copper-grounding wire connected to the lightning arrestor runs outside and down the light tower to its cement foundation, where it is connected to an earth ground terminal.

Parapet

There is a double-thickness door in the lower wall under one of the storm windows of the lantern, which provides a "crawl-through" opening to the parapet, encircling the lantern. The keeper used the parapet to clean and remove snow and ice accumulations from the storm windows, as well as observe weather conditions, vessel traffic, and marine activities.

The outside parapet "catwalk" and railing around the lightroom.
(Photo by the author)

Finials

Five decretive-type finials mounted on parapet railing posts were replaced in the 1900s with finials approximately six inches high and resembling miniature lighthouses.

A finial on one of the five railing posts of the parapet.
(Photo by the author)

There are only two other lighthouses in the United States equipped with similar "lighthouse" finials on their "catwalk" railing posts: West Chop lighthouse on Martha's Vineyard, Massachusetts, and Nubble Light in York, Maine.

Emergency Light Beacon

After electricity was used to light the Nobska Light tower, a standby light beacon with a red sector was necessary to provide a navigational light during power outages. The light beacon is mounted on the south side of the parapet railing approximately one foot below the focal plane of the main light. The light beacon faces Vineyard Sound with a luminous range of several miles. The beacon is battery-operated and automatically turns on whenever a power outage affects the light tower.

Nobska's emergency light beacon with built-in red sector.
(Photo by the author)

Lightroom

A seven-step iron ladder fastened against the wall of the watch room leads to a trapezoidal-shaped plywood hatch door in the ceiling for access to the lightroom.

Seven-step metal ladder in the watch room provides
access into the lightroom.
(Photo by the author)

Hatch door at the top of the ladder provides
access into the lightroom.
(Photo by the author)

The ten-sided lightroom is approximately eight feet in diameter and is enclosed with ten storm glass windows secured with iron vertical astragal framing. Three of the storm glass windows are covered with aluminum panels to block the light from residential areas.

Installing the Fifth-Order Fresnel Lens

The fifth-order lens and oil lamp previously used in the original lighthouse were transferred and installed in the lightroom of the new light tower. The lens was mounted on a pedestal centered on the floor and provides a focal plane of eighty-seven feet.[12]

Lamp Changer and Flasher

During the mid-1950s, an automatic lamp changer with flasher was added to cause the light to flash every few seconds.[13] The electrical circuitry was modified on June 16, 1959, to time the light to flash every six seconds.[14] The device was replaced with a Crouse-Hinds two-position automatic lamp changer with flasher no. FL-1214, using two one-thousand-watt 2C-5 T-20 lamps—one was marked "primary" and one marked "tripped." The standby lamp was positioned to landside to avoid blocking the active lamp. The bulb was turned on one hour before sunset and turned off at dusk. The electrical power panel for the circuitry was mounted on the watch room wall.

In February 2000, the US Lighthouse Service determined the 1000 watts was costly and unnecessary and replaced the no. CG2P (two-position, 1,000 watts) lamp changer with a no. CG4P (four-po-

---

[12] Surveyed on May 20–22 and June 22–26, 1886 on blueprint dated May 22, 1886. This blueprint stipulates the focal plane to be eighty-nine feet. However, all documents reviewed during research show the focal plane to be eighty-seven feet. The author believes the blueprint may be in error.

[13] A flashing light is lit for a short period, then off for a long period as opposed to an occulting light, which is lit for a long period, then off for a short period.

[14] National Archives at Boston in Waltham, Massachusetts, letter July 23, 1959, and legal notices no. 47, 44, 39, 31.

sition, 250 watts). The new lamp changer decreased the luminous range of the white light fifteen nautical miles to thirteen nautical miles and red light from twelve nautical miles to eleven nautical miles. However, the operating efficiency and cost-effectiveness were considerable. The two 1,000-watt lamps cost $125, versus $45 for the four 250-watt lamps.[15]

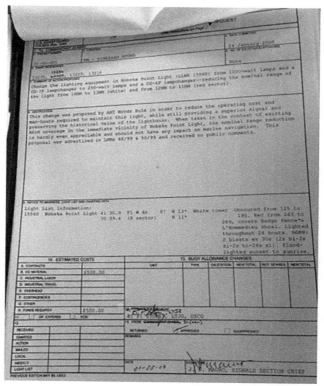

Government request to modify the lamp changer and lamps.
(National Archives, Washington, DC)

The arrangement was designed to prevent any of the three standby lamps from blocking the active lamp. The cost for the mod-

---

[15] Based on letter of recommendation, dated August 19, 1999, SA. Lucey, USCG, and change request dated January 24, 2000.

ification was $500. The four-position lamp changer with four 250-watt lamps and flasher is presently used in the lightroom.

Four 250-watt lamps in the automatic lamp-rotating device.
The active lamp is lit, and the remaining
three lamps are on standby.
(Photo by the author)

The 250-watt tubular-shaped bulbs are approximately three-eighth-inch diameter by one and a half inches long.
(Photo by the author)

The US Coast Guard schedules visit to Nobska Light every several months to conduct preventive maintenance on all equipment. During their visits, they generally replace one burned-out bulb in the automatic bulb rotating device and seldom need to replace two. Should an active bulb burn out, the mechanism automatically and quickly rotates to the next available bulb, and the USCG is notified.

Note that the active (lit) bulb is positioned vertically. This is important because the maximum amount of light waves from this bulb travel horizontally *directly* to the lens and outward. The minimum amount of light waves from this bulb travel vertically to refracting prisms of the lens and sent horizontally and outward. The benefits of a *vertically* mounted bulb inside a lens result in a very effective and efficient lamp for lighthouse purposes.

Air Ventilators

Five adjustable brass air vents—approximately eight inches in diameter, evenly spaced in, and along the lower half of the wall around the lightroom—allowed the keepers to manually regulate the flow of outside air entering the lightroom. These air vents were designed to prevent water and sand from entering the lightroom, which could otherwise destroy the lens.

One of five adjustable brass air vents in the wall around the lightroom.[16]
(Photo by the author)

---

[16] Note that in the photo, the center adjustment knob and the rotator disc are missing. However, the stationary portion seems to be authentic.

Proper adjustment of the air vents was very important to assure the oil lamp would burn evenly, brightly, and with a minimal amount of smoke.

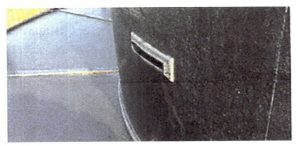

Outside view an air vent from the parapet.
(Photo by the author)

Install the Red Sector

A red sector was installed in 1888 to filter a section of Nobska's light to appear red. It's intent was to warn mariners sailing toward Nobska of the dangerous L'Hommediu and Hedge Fence Shoals in Vineyard Sound.[17]

Spillover from white light to red, and red to white, was inherent to the red-sector design during this time. However, modifications made by the USCG in the early 1960s resolved the "spillover" problem and led to a design using a red translucent panel installed over one of the ten storm windows of the lantern. The red-sector panel was positioned to show the white light as a flashing red light between 083 degrees and 109 degrees covering a 26 degree angle across rocks and shoals mentioned above. Mariners sailing on a westbound course toward Nobska light will see the flashing red light between 263 and 289 degrees.

---

[17] Blueprint dated May 22, 1888 shows the red sector angle to be 30 degrees 4 minutes. L'Hommedieu and Hedge Fence Shoals are on Vineyard Sound approximately fifteen miles east of Nobska light, and between West Chop light on Martha's Vineyard and the Cape Cod mainland.

Shoals

L'Hommedieu and Hedge Fence Shoals

Hedge Fence Shoal runs south of L'Hommedieu shoal. The western end of both shoals are approximately 4.3 miles east of Nobska light and continue east for another ten miles. The shoals are on Vineyard Sound between East Chop light on Martha's Vineyard, and Washburn Island on the mainland of Cape Cod. The north side of L'Hommedieu shoal is approximately fifteen feet deep. Near the western end of Hedge Fence Shoal the depth is approximately twenty feet. The eastern half of both shoals are in Nantucket Sound while the western half are in Vineyard Sound.

Translucent "red sector" panel presently
in the Nobska Lightroom.
(Photo by the author)

Upgrade to a Fourth-Order Fresnel Lens

In December 1888, the US Lighthouse Commission replaced the fifth-order lens at Nobska with a more powerful fourth-order lens. The oil lamp was upgraded to a brighter and more powerful lamp. A different size of lampstand may have been installed to accommodate the need for a taller lamp chimney. The new and more powerful lens and lamp increased the luminous range in dense fog and other conditions of poor visibility.

A more powerful fourth-order lens replaced the fifth-order
lens in 1888, and a red sector was added for the lens.
(Inspection report no. 120, National Archives, Washington, DC).

Oil Consumption

Due to the new larger and more powerful oil lamp installed with the new fourth-order lens, oil consumption increased from one hundred fifty-five gallons per year to two hundred forty-three gallons per year, 0.67 gallons per night—a thirty-six percent increase.

Fourth-order Fresnel lens.
(Photo by the author)

Upgrade the Oil Lamp

The oil lamp was replaced in 1914 with a brighter incandescent oil vaporizer (IOV)[18] lamp, which increased luminous range during poor visibility conditions. The IOV lamp mixed kerosene with air under pressure by means of an integral hand-operated pump with pressure gauge. Pressurized air typically lasted several hours.

---

[18] National Archives, Washington, DC, inspection report dated October 18, 1961. The chips and cracks found on the Fresnel fourth lens today were due to intensive heat caused by the IOV lamp. Invented in 1901.

The pressurized mixture created a fine mist that soaked a mantle. When lit, the mantle produced a brilliant and powerful white light similar to lamps used today for camping.

Damages to the Lens

Based on logbook entries by the keepers, *"Damages to the lens were due to flare-ups caused by intense heat from the IOV lamp." "The reliable Aladdin lamp with chimney continues to be used for back-up emergencies."*[19] Similar lamps were used every day in the keepers' dwellings as well.

The "reliable" Aladdin oil lamp.

---

[19] Electrical power outages may have been the reason the Nobska keeper used the standby IOV lamp despite its danger and destructiveness.

Keepers' logbook entries[20]

Electrical power outages may have been the reason the Nobska keeper used the standby IOV lamp despite its danger and destructiveness.

February 8, 1914	The flame from the IOV lamp flared up. The lamp was replaced.
February 16, 1914	McAffe had trouble with the new IOV lamp, switched back to old lamp.
February 25, 1914	Excessive heat from the IOV lamp caused a piece of the glass prism to fall out.
March 14, 1914	Vapor lamp flared up, melted solder on lamp fitting. Replaced with oil lamp. Keeper repaired vapor lamp then put back in service.
April 12, 1914	Vapor lamp flared up, used oil lamp.
February 18, 1916	Vapor lamp flared up.
September 19, 1916	One prism fell out from lens.
December 28, 1916	Vaporizer lamp flared up, smoked tower, cracked a prism.

Lantern Windows Covered

As a result of complaints from neighbors, three of the ten lantern windows around the lightroom facing residential homes were covered from inside the lantern with aluminum panels to block the powerful light from 305 degrees to 15 degrees (obscured neighbor's view from 125 degrees to 195 degrees). A Nobska Coast Guard keeper at the time told a Cape Cod Times reporter, "We also had

---

[20] National Archives, Washington, DC.

some neighbors complain about the light, but we just blocked out some panels and it doesn't bother them anymore."[21]

Watch Room

A thirty-three-step iron spiral stairway with balusters and hand-railing attached to the interior brick-lined wall follows the curvature of the wall from the ground-level to the fourth-level watch room. Nobska's light worked on a fixed light principle. However, some lighthouses were provided with clockworks attached to the base of the lens. The keeper would wind the clockworks every four to six hours.

As the lens rotates, the bull's-eye panels of the lens would appear as a flashing light to mariners. Flashing lights were used to help mariners identify lighthouses in their area and thus establish a fix.[22]

---

[21] Craig Little, "Setting Up Lighthouse Keeping," *Cape Cod Times*, February 13, 1983.

[22] The design of the Nobska Light tower was typical of many lighthouses that inherently allowed for clockworks. However, the author believes that Nobska Light was never configured to flash its light. Documents or evidence to suggest otherwise have not been found.

Thirty-three-step iron spiral stairway from ground level
to the watch room. Interior wall is brick lined.
(Photo by the author)

Bricks were laid to form a curved wall.
(Photo by the author)

One Italianate-style sash window is located on the ground level and two similar windows located strategically to provide daylight along the stairway to the watch room. The keeper stored lamp oil in this closet.

Oil storage closet in the watch room.
(Photo by the author)

However, during storms and conditions of poor visibility, an additional supply of oil was stored in the closet to keep the lamp burning continuously, day and night. The watch room was primarily used by the keeper for observing weather conditions, marine traffic, and marine activities on Vineyard Sound through four porthole windows, hence the name "watch room." Two of the porthole windows are fixed, and two are provided with hinged lock-handle mechanisms to facilitate opening from the inside to clean and to remove snow and ice accumulations.

One of the four porthole windows in the watch room.
(Photo by the author)

Lighthouse Floors

Constant foot traffic by keepers on cement or wood floors any-where in a light tower would cause worn-off particles to become air-borne and potentially scratch the Fresnel lens. For this reason, ladders and flooring in the parapet, lightroom, watch room, and entrance level were all made of metal.

Keepers' Dwelling

The keepers' dwelling and the light tower were built at the same time in 1876. The wood frame keepers' dwelling was a one-and-a-half-story structure, measuring thirty-seven feet three inches across the front and thirty-seven feet seven inches across the back and twenty-eight feet five inches across one side and twenty-eight feet six inches across opposite side (author's measurements), approximately 1,650 square feet with full basement. The dwelling was located approximately twenty-five feet east of the light tower and was built for $9,000.[23]

---

[23] Massachusetts Historical Commission, 80 Boylston Street, Boston, Massachusetts, 02116, dated July 24, 1981, file 87001483.pdf.

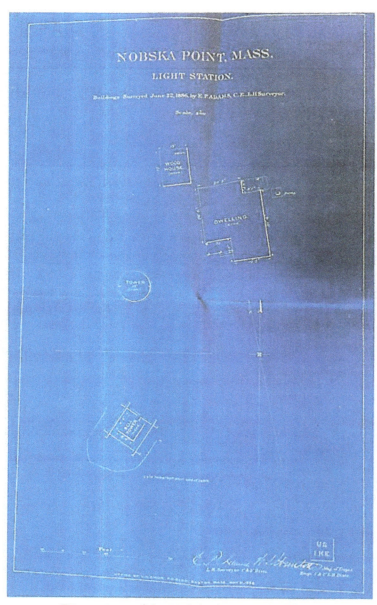

Dimensions of the Nobska keepers' dwelling.
(Drawing May 31, 1888, surveyed June 22, 1886)

During a thunderstorm on Wednesday morning, August 21, 1895, the dwelling, occupied by Nobska keeper Oliver Nickerson, was struck by lightning. Part of the chimney was knocked down, and several holes were made in different parts of the dwelling, but fortunately, no one was hurt.[24]

Walkway/Cistern

A covered walkway from the keepers' dwelling to the light tower was added in 1899 to provide the keeper with protection from the weather. A cistern was also installed during the same year.[25]

Inspection report no. 162: Covered walkway built in 1899.
(National Archives, Washington, DC)

Keeper Logbook Entries[26]

These entries show the new walkway was painted on an average of every two years. The walkway was removed during the mid-1960s.[27]

April 23, 1915	Painted covered walkway.
September 26, 1918	Painted walkway.
March 12, 1919	Painted walkway.
April 10, 1920	Painted walkway.
June 15, 1923	Painted walkway.
March 3, 1925	Painted walkway.

---

[24] *Hyannis Patriot*, August 26, 1895.
[25] The "added" cistern apparently was a replacement. An earlier inspection report no. 88 in chapter 1 explains repairs made to a cistern in 1868.
[26] National Archives, Washington, DC.
[27] Dates will be available in future editions.

All Lights Out!

During the Spanish-American War from April 21, 1898, to December 10, 1898, for the first time in United States history, President William McKinley ordered all lights, which can be seen from the sea, extinguished at night as a precaution.

Second Keepers' Dwelling Was Added

Due to heavy vessel traffic through the Woods Hole passage, the government hired George Cameron in 1905 to be the assistant keeper for head keeper Oliver Nickerson. The government built a one-and-a-half-story, twenty-seven-foot-by-twenty-eight-foot second keepers' dwelling for a cost of $6,000.

The dwelling was attached to the north side of the existing keepers' dwelling at the first level. The two dwellings shared a wall on the first level. However, for privacy purposes, they were not connected at the second level. There were three bedrooms, a kitchen, and a living room in each dwelling. The two families could move between their dwellings through two doors at the back porch.

Head keeper Oliver Nickerson and his family moved into the newer and larger dwelling while the new assistant keeper George Cameron occupied the smaller original dwelling.[28]

Improvements to the Keepers' Dwellings

On September 30, 1957, the old and deteriorated coal-fired boilers in both of the keepers' dwellings were replaced with new oil-fired furnaces at a total cost of $4,275.[29] The new furnaces were equipped with thermostats in each dwelling and a one-thousand-gallon underground oil tank to serve both dwellings.

---

[28] Brian Melville, "Three Nickersons Play Roles in Nobska Point Light." Mr. Brian Melville Nickerson was a tour guide at Nobska Light and a distant cousin to keeper Oliver Nickerson.

[29] National Archives at Boston in Waltham, Massachusetts.

In 1966, vinyl siding replaced the original Cape Cod cedar shingles on the two keepers' dwellings despite dissatisfaction from the Historical Society and complaints from neighbors to retain the cedar shingles. Years later, at the request of the Woods Hole Historical Museum, the keeper's homes were both converted back to Cape Cod cedar shingles. However, neighbors again complained, but this time, to retain the vinyl siding!

While USCG Commander Peter Collom and his family were living in the keepers' dwellings at Nobska from 1985 until 1987, Commander Collom remodeled the two keepers' dwellings to join them as one. He removed a load-bearing wall between the kitchens in the two buildings and installed a boxed-in beam to support the load.

After Nobska was automated, five other USCG commanders occupied the Nobska home. However, in 2014, the house was deemed in need of serious maintenance and, therefore, discontinued as a residence.

Electricity Coming to Nobska

November 26, 1917	A telephone equipment building was erected at Nobska station.
June 8, 1918	Electric company installed utility poles at Nobska Point.

Nobska Lit by Electricity!

Electrical power became available on Cape Cod in 1910, but it wasn't until June 8–10, 1918, that the electric company installed utility poles and provided electric power to the Nobska Light Station. The oil lamp in the light tower was replaced on January 7, 1919, with a 150-watt light bulb. On the following night, on January 8, the light tower was lit all night for the very *first* time.

The electric light bulb eliminated the need for kerosene and significantly increased visibility from eight nautical miles to twelve nautical miles during clear weather conditions. The following entries are from the keepers' logbooks before and after electricity was installed at the Nobska Light Station.[30]

After Electricity

These entries show that new severe problems surfaced in the lightroom as a result of using the newly installed electrical power. During this period, it seems that the new system of electrical power was vulnerable to having blackout and brownout situations caused by damages to transmission wiring between utility poles, substations, storms and wind, loose wiring connections, to mention a few. Reliable oil lamps were, apparently, always filled and kept close by and available in the event of such problems.

January 8, 1919	Light bulb in the lens lit all night long for the *first* time.
January 15–16, 1919	Keeper McAffe was on watch when the light bulb went out after midnight. He temporarily fixed it by hanging the bulb over the top and inside of the lens. (The author believes a fault may have occurred due to overheated wire connections.)
February 7, 1919	Bulb burned out from 9:30 to 10:00 p.m.
March 4, 1919	Bulb burned out, changed to vapor lamp.
April 12, 1919	Power outage, used oil vapor lamp remainder of the night.
August 14, 1919	Power outage at 1:30 a.m., used oil vapor lamp remainder of the night.
August 24, 1919	Power outage, used oil vapor lamp.
July 6, 1922	Power outage, used oil lamp.
August 7, 1922	Power outage.
May 1, 1924	Power outage.
October 16, 1926	Power outage, used vapor lamp.
January 11, 1927	Power outage, used oil vapor lamp.

---

[30] National Archives, Washington, DC.

Standby Generator

In 1935, a gasoline generator was apparently used to run the radio beacon transmitter equipment during power outages. During the 1950s, a fifteen-kilowatt consolidated diesel[31] backup generator powered the fog-signaling compressor and the light.

Keeper Osborne Hallett performing daily tests
of the backup generator in 1962.[32]

Power Outages

A battery backup system is used at Nobska, which automatically provides power to run the fog-signaling equipment, emergency light beacon, and the light tower during power outages. The backup

---

[31] Woods Hole Historical Museum document Form 152.171.
Inspection report October 18, 1961, National Archives at Boston in Waltham, Massachusetts.
National Archives at Boston in Waltham, Massachusetts, July 1949 emergency generator.
[32] Photo April 17, 1962 Falmouth Enterprise.

system consists of two banks of lead-acid batteries, a battery charger, and an inverter.

Backup power in the equipment building at Nobska.
Bottom: battery banks.
Top left: battery charger.
(Photo by the author)

Woodshed

The dimensions of the woodshed were thirteen feet by seventeen feet and located approximately fifty feet north-northeast of the light tower.[33]

The woodshed was removed in 1905 to make room for the addition of a second keepers' dwelling. A logbook entry suggested that a new woodshed was built at a later date.

---

[33] Blueprint no. 1225 sheet 1 of 2, surveyed June 22, 1886.

Keepers' Logbook Entry[34]

August 6, 1919, "Keeper removed goat stalls from the firewood shed."

Oil House

The oil house was used to store whale oil and kerosene for use in the lightroom and the keepers' dwellings. It was of wood construction and located approximately one hundred feet north-northwest of the light tower.[35]

The wooden oil house was replaced in 1901 with a more permanent and safe brick construction at a cost of $1,000.[36] It was built at a safe distance of approximately 150 feet east of the light tower. The measurements are ten feet two inches by twelve feet one inch (author's measurements).

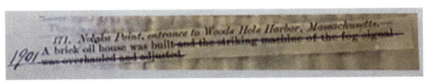

Inspection report no. 171: Brick oil house built in 1901.
(National Archives, Washington, DC)

For further safety, windows were not included in the new oil house, and the roof was made of slate. There is a ventilation opening on the south wall of the building above the entrance door. The oil house also served as a paint storage locker.

---

[34] National Archives, Washington, DC.

[35] Blueprint no. 1225 sheet 1 of 2, surveyed June 22, 1886.

[36] National Archives at Boston in Waltham, Massachusetts, letter October 18, 1961.

Keepers' Logbook Entries[37]

October 31, 1913, ten-gallon cases of mineral oil from ship stored in oil house. Between 1926 and 1928, an underground kerosene tank[38] was installed next to the oil house.

October 16, 1926	Painted the brick oil house red.
1928	Emptied three hundred gallons into the new kerosene tank.
September 22, 1948	Painted the brick oil house brown.
December 30, 1948	Received two fifty-gallon containers of kerosene for the oil house.
January 1949	Placed two hundred gallons of kerosene in tank in oil house.
As of October 1961	The brick oil house had a slate roof.[39]

Brick oil house built in 1901.
(Photo by the author)

---

[37] National Archives, Washington, DC.

[38] National Archives at Boston in Waltham, Massachusetts.

[39] National Archives at Boston in Waltham, Massachusetts.

Henhouse

Blueprint dated May 22, 1888, shows the hencoop approximately two hundred feet north-northeast of the light tower at the northern boundary of the Nobska property line. In August 1919, Assistant keeper Robert McAffe built a new hencoop. Although I was unable to find documentation, Mr. McAffe may have built the hencoop close to his dwelling for convenience.

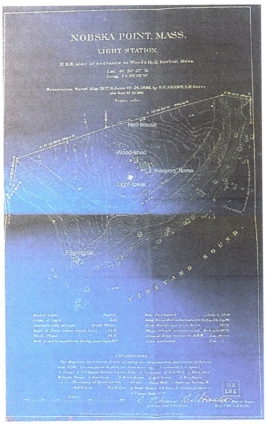

Henhouse was located two hundred feet northeast of the light tower. Surveyed on May 20–22, June 22–26, and September 1886.
Blueprint dated May 22, 1888.
(*National Archives, Washington, DC*)

Pigpen

Assistant keeper Robert McAffe also built a pigpen according to logbook entries. However, documents showing its location on the Nobska property could not be found.

Keepers' Logbook Entry[40]

May 29, 1918	Assistant keeper Robert McAffe built a pigpen.
May 24, 1919	Principal keeper George Cameron installed new posts for the pigpen.

Flagpole and Floodlights

The keepers' logbook shows that a flagpole was installed on December 16, 1949, and during the mid-1960s, seven 150-watt floodlights were installed to illuminate the light tower from sunset to sunrise. The floodlights were controlled to turn on and off with the light tower.[41]

Storm-warning flags were displayed in September 1968 during the daytime and lit by floodlights at night.[42]

Automation

The equipment that normally had to be manually turned on and off, such as the light in the lightroom and the fog-signaling controls, were fully automated in 1985. The light automatically turned on and off by means of light-sensing controls and the fog-signaling controls automatically detected fog or poor visibility conditions day or night then automatically turned on the audible fog signal. Automation eliminated the need for the US Coast Guard lighthouse keepers.

---

[40] National Archives, Washington, DC.
[41] National Archives at Boston in Waltham, Massachusetts.
[42] *Enterprise* newspaper, September 27, 1968.

Garage

Logbook entries revealed there have been several garages built at the Nobska station throughout its history.

Keepers' Logbook Entries[43]

The garage was painted on July 26, 1915. Then on July 11, 1922, a cement foundation was poured for a new garage. In 1931, an automobile garage was added with a foghorn attached, but the foghorn was later removed. As of 1968, the garage was used for automobiles and for storing groundskeeping equipment.[44]

---

[43] National Archives, Washington, DC.
[44] Research continues to develop a more detailed timeline.

⚓

CHAPTER 3

Nobska Lighthouse Keepers

Introduction

THE HEAD KEEPER at lighthouse stations was the boss. He or she planned the daily work, assigned duties, and worked in harmony with their assistant keepers. However, head keepers did not have disciplinary power, and they did not control pay increases or leave of absences. They could not terminate or transfer an assistant keepers' employment. Such authority was provided by the US Lighthouse Service, which was established in 1885.

Lighthouse keeper positions were politically appointed when their presidential candidates came into power. Requirements to become a lighthouse keeper was the keeper had to be at least eighteen years of age, able to read, and had to be married.[45] There were several women lighthouse keepers in America as well. Women performed the same duties as men but received half the pay and were not required to wear uniforms.

After the last civilian keeper Joseph Hindley retired at Nobska Light in 1973, the US Coast Guard Group Commander at Woods

---

[45] A comment made by Paul Gonyea USCG resident at Nobska appeared on January 2, 1985, *Cape Cod Times* by Lisa Martin, "Lighthouse Shines on Holidays": "*You need to be married to get lighthouse duty and since I was getting married soon, I thought I would apply. After I was married I moved into the lighthouse complex on Oct 16, 1984.*"

Hole, and the head keepers and their assistants, were assigned to live at Nobska for a specified term. They were required to provide free lighthouse tours to the public between Memorial Day and Labor Day. After the first USCG assignment at Nobska in 1985, the Nobska Light Station was automated and assistant keepers were no longer required.

The Nobska Keepers' Uniform

In 1884, the Lighthouse Board introduced dress uniforms for lighthouse keepers. Uniforms consisted of a coat, vest, trousers, and a cap. A double row of yellow metal buttons was on the front of the double-breasted coat, and a yellow metal lighthouse badge was on the cap. Keepers were authorized to wear sleeve insignias to indicate their length of service.

Requirements for Nobska Keepers

Can you imagine living and working at Nobska Lighthouse nearly two hundred years ago? On a typical day, the keeper would go out to the oil storage building, fill several five-gallon containers with an ample supply of oil, then return to the lighthouse. He would store the oil containers in the watch room closet.

He would bring lamps down from the lightroom to the watch room to fill with oil. He would trim the wicks, polish the reflectors, then realign lamps and reflector assemblies to produce maximum brightness. Uniforms were required to be worn by male lighthouse keepers at all times while on duty. If found not wearing his uniform, or not wearing it properly, he could be fined or even fired!

Routine polishing reflectors would often result in distorting their shapes. As a result, keepers had to "reshape" the parabolic reflectors. Keepers' duties included keeping the outside windows of the lantern clear during any weather conditions.

Keepers were held to strict rules mandated by the United States Lighthouse Service. If boats got in trouble, keepers were expected to assist. They also had to take care of nine buoys off Nobska Point, and when the weather became foggy, they had to activate the fog bell machinery. They had to mow and trim the lawn on the property, paint inside and outside their homes, as well as the lighthouse tower, and maintain windows and screens on all buildings.

The most important part of his duties was to maintain the oil lamps and keep them burning from dusk until after dawn. However, during storm conditions, such as a hurricane, the lamps had to be kept burning until the storm was over.

As of 1872, the government required lighthouse keepers to maintain logbooks and record daily activities, such as weather conditions, wind direction, wind speed, the time fog started and ended, the number of hours the foghorn was active, deliveries to the dwelling and tower, the time oil lamps were lit and extinguished, weather conditions, cloud formations, atmospheric conditions, shipwrecks, and oil consumption.[46]

They were also required to record the quantity and types of vessels that sailed passed Nobska Point as either private or commercial. For example, in 1829, there were approximately 10,000 vessels recorded, and during the month of November 1864, there were 833 vessels recorded. During a *single* day in 1865, keeper Frederic Ray recorded 188 vessels.

Nobska keepers were allowed to have their families with them in lighthouse dwellings year around. Handling lighthouse chores was a family effort with everyone working together.

Keepers' Instructions and Directions

Each lighthouse was issued a maintenance and instruction sheet on the care and operation of the lighting system to be posted in the lightroom. However, in 1851, lighthouse inspectors found most lighthouse keepers did not post their instructions. The US

---

[46] Logbooks read at the National Archives, Washington, DC, by the author revealed that although many requirements were accomplished, few were recorded.

Lighthouse Service provided official documents[47] to all lighthouse keepers, which included the following:

1. Clean glass windows inside and out.
2. Clean glass, fill oil lamps, and trim wicks every four hours.
3. Remove moisture from the interior of the oil lamps.
4. Silver-plated reflector fronts must be polished with rouge power only.
5. Brass parts must be cleaned weekly with Tripoli Powder mixed with waste oil.
6. Lightroom must be in perfect order by 10:00 a.m. daily.
7. Lamps shall be lit at sunset and extinguished at sunrise.
8. Responsible for the cleanliness, order, and condition of passages, stairs, roofs, water cisterns, wells, storage rooms, workshops, stables, and ashpits.
9. Responsible for local buoy channel markers.
10. Maintain daily logbooks.
11. Make winter oil lighter to stay liquid in the unheated watch room.
12. Carry oil from the storage building to the watch room for daily use.
13. Realign oil lamp and reflectors throughout the night for maximum brightness.
14. Adjust ventilators during the night to control ambient air to assure steady, clear, and bright flames.
15. Alternate watch in the lightroom every four hours throughout the night.
16. Store water buckets in a convenient place in the event of fire.
17. Repair dikes, roads, and drains leading to the lighthouse.

---

[47] Section 1 from official document *Directions to the Light Keeper of the United States Light Stations With Two or More Keepers.* Section 2 and section 16 from official document *Instructions to the Light Keeper of the United States Light Stations With One Keeper.* Section 3 from official document *Directions to the Light Keeper of the United States Light Stations With Two or More Keepers.*

18. Must not leave the premises except to draw salary and to attend worship.
19. Must be sober, industrious, orderly, and polite.
20. Must not have more than three visitors in the lightroom at any one time during the day. No one allowed after sunset.
21. Order all supplies.
22. Receive deliveries and provide unloading assistance.
23. Bring crewmembers and passengers to safety should their vessels get in trouble.
24. Wear the official uniform properly at all times while on duty.

Who Were the Nobska Lighthouse Keepers?

There were thirteen different civilian keepers at Nobska from 1829 to 1973. Oliver A. Nickerson was the longest keeper with thirty-seven years of service, and Joseph G. Hindley was the longest assistant keeper with twelve years of service. There were six US Coast Guard keepers from late 1973 to 1985, after which the lighthouse was automated and thus eliminating the need for keepers.

After 1985, US Coast Guard commanders became residents at Nobska Light. The following list includes civilian and US Coast Guard keepers, assistants, and their terms of service over the one-hundred-fifty-six-year period.

Head Keeper	Years	Assistant Keeper	Years
Peter Daggett 1829 to Summer 1849	20	Not required[48]	-

---

[48] Assistant keepers were not necessary at Nobska until vessel traffic became overwhelming in 1905. An assistant keeper was then hired, and a second dwelling was built.

William Davis July 1849 to 1853	4	Not required	-		
William Ferguson Jr. May 18, 1853, to December 18, 1861	8	Not required	-		
Frederic Ray December 18, 1861, to 1874 (Retired) Beginning salary $350/year Ending salary $500/year	13	Not required	-		
Oliver A. Nickerson September 28, 1874, to May 13, 1911	37	George I. Cameron[49] July 30, 1910, to May 13, 1911	1		
George I. Cameron May 14, 1911, to September 17, 1913	2	George T. Gustavus June 1, 1911, to September 17, 1913	2		
George L. Lyon September 17, 1913, to June 30, 1929	16	George T. Gustavus September 17, 1913, to September 23,1915	2		
		Robert M. McAfee 1915 to October 9, 1925	10		

---

[49] Because of Nobska Light, shipwrecks reduced significantly. Due to increased number of vessels sailing past Nobska, an assistant keeper was hired, and a second dwelling was built. George Cameron was Nobska's first assistant keeper.

		John M. Scharff October 17, 1925, to July 1, 1929	4
John M. Scharff July 1, 1929, to 1944	15	Waldo Leighton July 2, 1929, to 1939	10
		George T. Gustavus 1939 to 1941	2
		Ralph L. Sellers October 6, 1941, to 1944	3
Ralph L. Sellers 1944 to May 6, 1946	2	Unknown	2
John M. Scharff May 23, 1946, to 1955	9	Ralph L. Sellers May 7, 1946, to 1955	9
Osborne Earl Hallett[50] 1955 to January 1967	12	Joseph G. Hindley 1955 to January 1967	12
Donald Self, USCG 1967 to 1973	6	Joseph G. Hindley 1967 to 1973	6
Unknown, USCG 1973 to 1980	7	Unknown, USCG 1973 to 1980	7

---

[50] Osborne Earl Hallett was released from duty in 1967.

Gary Williams, USCG
February 13, 1980, 3
to July 1983

David Rivera, USCG
February 13, 1980, 3
to July 1983

Charles Tebo, USCG
1983 to 1985 2

Paul Gonyea, USCG
October 16, 2
1983, to 1985

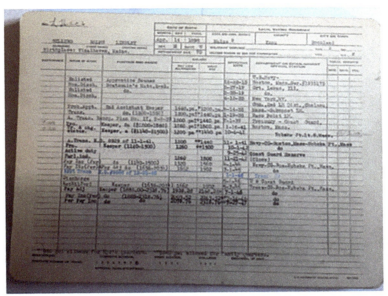

Service record (assignments and salary) for Nobska keeper
Ralph Lindsey Sellers.
(Courtesy United State Lighthouse Society [USLHS])

After Nobska Light was automated in 1985, six US Coast Guard commanders lived at Nobska Light to oversee operations until 2014.

US Coast Guard Residents at Nobska

Peter Collom
June 1985 to July 1987

Fredrick M. Hamilton
Year 1987 to 1989

Russell Webster
Year 1998 to August 1, 2001

James F. Murray
Year 2001 to 2003

Raymond J. Perry
Year 2003 to 2009

Verne D. Gifford
Year 2009 to 2014

Captain John T. Kondratowicz was the next USCG commander scheduled to live at Nobska Light for a three-year term. However, Coast Guard officials toured the keepers' dwellings and deemed them uninhabitable. Captain Kondratowicz did not become a resident, and no one has lived at the Nobska Light Station since 2014.

As more modern conveniences and automation became available, Nobska keepers were eventually phased out. The last civilian keeper at Nobska was Joseph Hindley, who retired in 1973. The last USCG keeper was Paul Gonyea, ending his tour of duty in 1985.

How Much Were Nobska Keepers Paid?

Lighthouse keepers throughout the United States were paid anywhere from $100 to $400 per year depending on the year, the length of service, and the location of the lighthouse.

The first keeper at Nobska was Peter Daggett from 1828 to 1849. Toward the end of his term, Mr. Daggett was paid $87.50 quarterly or $350 annually.[51]

---

[51] Payment document, National Archives, Washington, DC.

The beginning salary for Frederic Ray in 1861 was $350 per year, and the ending salary in 1874 was $500 per year. In 1867, the US Congress fixed the maximum pay scale for keepers at $600, a law that remained unchanged for fifty years.

The beginning salary for Ralph F. Sellers on October 6, 1941, was $1,440 per year, and the ending salary on May 7, 1946, was $1,902 per year.

Benefits for Keepers

As of 1916, Congress provided that lightkeepers and assistant keepers shall be entitled to medical relief benefits at hospitals and other facilities of the public health service without charge. Retirement benefits were added in 1918. Congress provided disability retirement within the Lighthouse Service in 1925 and authorized the purchase of rubber boots, oilskins, and related items for use while engaging in lighthouse duties requiring such equipment. Congress repealed the law providing a ration allowance for keepers. However, salaries were increased.

A year later, Congress extended the benefits to keepers that were located on isolated (stag) lights, and in 1930, Congress provided that during active service, keepers were entitled to medical relief at hospitals and other facilities of the public health service and to continue such medical relief after retirement.

Awards

On December 29, 1967, Nobska keepers Osborne Earl Hallett and Joseph G. Hindley Jr. were awarded Albert Gallatin Certificates by Capt. Frederick J. Hancox, commanding officer USCG, Woods Hole.[52] These men were among the last civilian lighthouse keepers in New England.

---

[52] Frederick J. Hancox, "Falmouth's Past," *Enterprise*, September 27, 1968.

Left: Nobska keeper Osborne Earl Hallett.
Center: Nobska assistant keeper Joseph G. Hindley.
(Photo courtesy Falmouth Enterprise)

Rescue Boat

Based on the location of the Nobska Light Station, a boat was provided for keepers to use for rescue purposes.

Keepers' Logbook Entries[53]

       1948   Greased the boat hoist.

Interesting Stories Involving Nobska Keepers

Peter Daggett

Peter Daggett was a veteran of the War of 1812. On November 1, 1838, the US Navy praised Peter Daggett for his reputation and orderliness at Nobska Lighthouse. However, Mr. Daggett was removed from his head keeper position in 1849 because he was a Democrat.

---

[53] National Archives, Washington, DC.

Frederic Ray

"Ellery Wright lived with his stepfather, Nobska keeper Frederic Ray, during the 1860s and occasionally assisted in caring for the lighthouse until he was twenty years at which time he moved out."[54]

Frederic Ray

Recorded 833 vessels passing by Nobska light during 1864.

Oliver A. Nickerson

During a thunderstorm on Wednesday morning, August 21, 1895, the dwelling of Nobska keeper, Oliver Nickerson, was struck by lightning. Part of the chimney was knocked down, and several holes were made in different parts of the dwelling, but fortunately, no one was hurt.[55]

Oliver A. Nickerson and George I. Cameron

On Saturday, May 13, 1911, Nobska head lighthouse keeper Oliver Nickerson went to relieve his assistant keeper George Cameron for breakfast, who had been attending the fog-signaling apparatus during a fog. However, after breakfast, assistant Cameron returned to the fog-signaling apparatus, where he found Oliver Nickerson dead in his chair due to heart failure.[56] Mr. Cameron was promoted to head keeper on May 13, 1911, upon the death of head keeper Oliver Nickerson.[57]

---

[54] From the book *Representative Men and Old Families of Southeastern Massachusetts*, page 1607.
[55] *Hyannis Patriot News*, August 26, 1895.
[56] *Decatur Herald*, May 18, 1930.
[57] Yarmouth Register, May 27, 1911.

George I. Cameron

In August 1911, Boston-bound steamer *Bunker Hill*, with three hundred passengers, ran aground in Woods Hole passage by Nobska light. Nobska head keeper George Cameron summoned for help, and all passengers were rescued.

George I. Cameron

While George Cameron was head keeper at Nobska, Herman, the son of former head keeper Oliver Nickerson, was allowed to remain at Nobska light as a border. A newspaper reported that in October 1911, Cameron's wife took their six children and ran off with Herman to parts unknown.

Robert M. McAfee

On July 7, 1924, during a thick fog, Nobska keeper Robert M. McAfee was able to get a troubled yacht off the rocks at the entrance to Woods Hole.

John M. Scharff

Head keeper John Scharff had a long thirty-year stay as a Nobska keeper. Early one morning in May 1930, the fifteen-thousand-ton steel freighter *Kearny*, with about twenty-five men aboard, ran into rocks near Nobska Light in a light fog. Keeper Scharff quickly phoned the Woods Hole US Coast Guard station, and aid was hurried to the vessel. There were no injuries.[58]

---

[58] Sandwich Observer, June 6, 1911.

John M. Scharff and Waldo Leighton

In August 1935, Nobska head keeper John Scharff and assistant keeper Waldo Leighton rescued a man near Nobska light who had fallen overboard from his sailboat in a squall.

John M. Schraff and George T. Gustavus

Assistant keeper George Gustavus's daughter moved into Nobska Light at the age of sixteen. Before moving to Nobska, she lived on Bird Island off Marion, Massachusetts, where her mother and younger brother tragically died during the Hurricane of 1938. For this reason, she liked living on the mainland at Nobska Light. She married head keeper John Schraffs's son John, whom she met while living at Nobska.

John M. Scharff

John Scharff entered the military reserves in 1944 then returned to his head keeper position at Nobska in 1946.

John M. Scharff

On September 11, 1947, head keeper John Scharff caught his right arm in the foghorn compressor belt while oiling a pulley. His arm was broken, and he had to be taken to the Tobin Hospital Emergency Room.

Joseph G. Hindley

Joseph G. Hindley was believed to be the last civilian lighthouse keeper in New England.

Events Involving Nobska

Rescues

The power catboat *Eleanor* had a thrilling experience during a storm Tuesday night, January 12, 1915, in Vineyard Sound. They left Woods Hole late in the afternoon, and when nearly to the harbor, the engine stopped. They decided to anchor for the night, but the gale steadily increased, and they were forced to get underway.

They tried to make Falmouth Harbor but failed. Captain George Sherburne of the fishing steamer *Ripple* was in Falmouth Harbor and observed the situation. He quickly put out to their rescue but was unable to overtake the *Eleanor*. When *Eleanor* was abreast of Nobska Light, the lighthouse crew discovered her and sent word to the US fishing steamer *Phalarope* at Woods Hole. *Phalarope* soon overtook *Eleanor* and brought her to safety.[59]

Rescues

During a thick fog on July 7, 1924, the Nobska keeper was able to get a troubled yacht off the rocks at the entrance to Woods Hole.[60]

Accident

Attempts to refloat the fifty-two-foot Provincetown sloop *Elmer S* from a sandbar off Nobska Light in December 1931 have been abandoned, and salvage operations have started. The *Elmer S* struck a submerged rock and went ashore to escape from sinking as water poured into a gash torn in her hull.[61]

---

[59] *Hyannis Patriot*, January 18, 1915.
[60] *Decatur Herald*, May 18, 1930.
[61] Yarmouth Register, December 12, 1931.

Stories

Story as told by Peter and Edna Collom: Edna and I lived at Nobska Light from 1985 until 1987. I was serving my tour of duty at Nobska Point as the US Coast Guard commander of the Woods Hole district. Sometime in early July 1985, I awoke to find the weather conditions quite foggy. It was our first foggy night at Nobska, and I couldn't see Martha's Vineyard!

Down the stairs, out the back door to the attached porch, and I flipped the fog switch to On. No sound from the foghorn! Back in the house, up the stairs, I said, "Edna, the foghorn isn't working."

"Oh, I forgot to tell you, Peter. They moved the switch to the fog equipment building!"

Down the stairs, out the back door, down the cement steps, into the fog equipment building, flip the switch to On. Yes!

Cesspool

A cesspool was a part of the original lighthouse station. The only document found was the keepers' logbook, which confirms that a cesspool was at Nobska in 1948.

CHAPTER 4

Fog Signal and Radio Beacon

I SAY, "LIGHTHOUSE lights and fog signals work well together…
When the light can't be seen, the fog signal might be heard."

Introduction

There have been six different fog-signaling technologies used
at the Nobska Light Station over the past 143 years from the first
fog bell installed in 1875 to the current state-of-the-art remote-controlled electronic system installed in 2018. With advances in fog-signaling technologies came an increase in efficiency, cost-effectiveness,
improved sound quality, and distances covered.

First Fog Signal at Nobska Station

The first fog-signaling system at the Nobska Light Station was a
bell. It was erected in 1875 and consisted of a bell attached to striking
machinery. The bell was mounted on a triangular-shaped wooden
skeletal frame and attached to the striking machinery located inside
an eight-foot-four-inch-by-nine-foot-four-inch wooden house at the
base of the frame. The house provided the striking machinery with
protection against the weather and stormy seas. The keeper would
manually wind and activate the striking machinery during conditions of poor visibility.

Information on the number of bell sounds, the interval between bell sounds, and the length of time the striking machinery could run after it was wound could not be found or does not exist.[62]

The fog bell was manually activated during dense fog conditions and whenever visibility was poor. Martha's Vineyard Island, being only a few miles from Nobska light, keepers were known to have said, "I activate the fog bell whenever Martha's Vineyard cannot be seen." The fog bell was located approximately 250 feet south of the lighthouse on the banks of Vineyard Sound.[63]

Original fog bell skeletal tower at Nobska built in 1875.
Small building inside the tower housed
striking machinery. Note bell on the tower.
(*Photo: National Archives, Washington, DC*)

---

[62] Research is continuing, and answers will appear in following editions of this book.
[63] See blueprint dated May 22, 1886, and blueprint no. 1225 in chapter 3, "New Nobska Light Station [1876]."

Typical Daboll fog bell striking machinery.
(Photo courtesy Lighthouse Establishment [LHE])

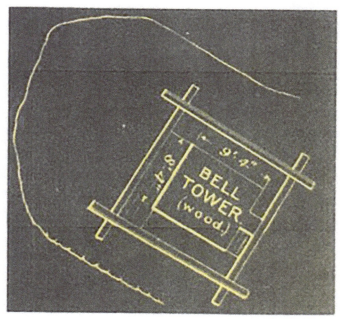

Section of the blueprint showing the size of the wooden
house for striking machinery.
(Surveyed on June 22, 1886; drawing on May 31, 1888).

New Machinery

By 1888, the old and worn-out striking machinery was replaced with new machinery. The striking mechanism was set to strike two bell sounds every thirty seconds.

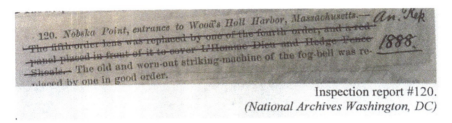

Inspection report #120.
(National Archives Washington, DC)

Seawall

In 1892, a stone seawall, five feet thick, five feet high, and a hundred feet long, was built on the shore of Vineyard Sound to protect the fog house and equipment against damage from weather and stormy seas.

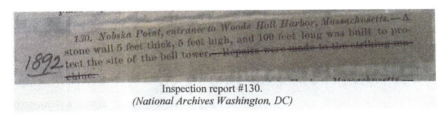

Inspection report #130.
(National Archives Washington, DC)

Decades later, on November 30, 1955, a new seawall was built to protect the road between the Nobska Light Station and the waters of Vineyard Sound from erosion.

Machinery House

The house for the striking machinery was replaced in 1900 with a new house.

> *166. Nobska Point, entrance to Woods Hole Harbor, Massachu-
> setts.—A new house was built for the striking machine for the fog-
> 1900 bell and the machinery overhauled and put in order; the bell tower
> was strengthened, ~~the site was protected from the sea by a stone~~
> ~~apron; about 95 running feet of bridge was built, and the fuel house~~
> ~~and barn were rebuilt.~~*

Inspection report no. 166: A new house was built in
1900 for the striking machine.
(National Archives, Washington, DC)

Modern Fog Tower

In 1907, the fog bell tower was replaced with a more modern
version.

Modern Nobska fog bell tower built in 1907.
(Photo: National Archives, Washington, DC)

Nobska Point, Mass. L.H.

> *181. Nobska Point, northerly side of Vineyard Sound, Massa-
> chusetts.—A fog-bell tower of modern type was built and various re-* 1907
> *pairs were made.*

Inspection report no. 181
(National Archives, Washington, DC)

A bell…cannot be considered an efficient fog signal on the seacoast. In calm weather it cannot
be heard half the time at a distance greater than
one mile, while in rough water the noise of the
surf will drown its sound to seaward altogether.
(General Duanne, US Army)

Fog Whistle

Despite protests from the local community, the US Lighthouse
Board installed a steam-driven compressed air whistle in 1911 to
replace the fog bell and its machinery. However, the fog bell remained
as a backup system until June 10, 1918, when the bell, machinery,
and house, were removed.

*Note: Information on the fog whistle was obtained from confirmed
documents. However, decades after the fog whistle was removed, logbook
entry, dated May 12, 1945, reference to the "whistle building" continued.*

Fog Trumpet Reed

A fog trumpet reed system, powered by a steam-driven air compressor, replaced the fog whistle. The reed in the fog trumpet was
made from steel ten inches long and two and one-fourth inches wide
and tapered in thickness from one inch at the fixed end to one-half
inch at the free end, thereby, resembling a musical "trumpet."

*Note: Information on the fog trumpet reed was obtained from
confirmed documents. Further details with dates will appear in future
editions.*

Fog Reed

A vibrating steel-reed fog-signaling device, powered by an electric air compressor, was installed in 1938 to replace the trumpet reed.
This new device provided three blasts every thirty seconds. However,
after the September 1944 hurricane, it was rendered useless due to
severe storm damage and was sold to a local resident for $10.

Keepers' Logbook Entries

October 14, 1911   Cleaned brass in fog signal house.
June 10, 1918   Removed fog bell house and machinery.
October 15, 1918   Installed water pipes to the bell tower.
May 10–12, 1919   Removed the fog bell tower.
March 27, 1929   Fog signal building painted red.
March 29, 1945   Start building a new fog-horn building.
July 26, 1947   The fog mechanism and gears were greased.
December 1947   Greased bell mechanism and gears.
July 11, 1948   The fog mechanism and gears were greased.

Equipment Building

Due to erosion and frequent water surges, in early November 1948, a new brick building was built[64] to accommodate the fog-signaling equipment and radio beacon transmitter equipment. The building is located seventy-five feet east of the keepers' dwelling.

New equipment building built in 1948.
(Photo by the author)

---

[64] National Archives at Boston in Waltham, Massachusetts, letter January 13, 1948.

The new equipment building measures twenty-six feet six inches by twenty-two feet five inches (author's measurements) and was built at a cost of $1,000.[65]

Air Diaphragm

On November 30, 1948, a new diaphragm fog system replaced the reed system.[66] The new fog system operated by means of an electric air compressor. When activated, compressed air passed between two fourteen-inch diameter metal discs to create the sound.

Two thirteen-foot-long-by-five-foot-diameter black tanks stored the compressed air. Both fog equipment and tanks were located in the equipment building. The fog controls were set to sound three blasts through dual horns every thirty seconds. The sound could be heard from twelve miles out to sea. A Kohler standby gasoline generator was used to back up the air compressor during power outages. The total cost for the new system was $21,850.[67]

A plywood baffle was installed in July 1949 to dampen the blasts in response to complaints from local neighbors.[68]

On November 30, 1955, a temporary air siren inside a wooden frame using the existing horns was installed while a new seawall to protect the fog equipment[69] was being built.

An inspection report, dated October 18, 1961, noted that the fog signal was a Leslie Tyfon A-300 type[70] 300 mm diaphragm (twelve inches in diameter). This device used three diaphragms each

---

[65] Massachusetts Historical Commission, 80 Boylston Street, Boston, Massachusetts, 02116, dated July 24, 1981, file 87001483.pdf. National Achieves at Boston letter, dated July 18, 1961.

[66] Notice to Mariners no109, National Archives at Boston Waltham, Massachusetts.

[67] National Archives at Boston in Waltham, Massachusetts, letter, January 3, 1948.

[68] National Archives at Boston in Waltham, Massachusetts.

[69] National Archives at Boston and Woods Hole Historical Museum Form 152.114.

[70] National Archives at Boston and Woods Hole Historical Museum Form 152.114.

was three-sixteenth-inch thick. The distance covered by the sound coming from this device was rated at six to seven miles.

Keeper Osborne Earl Hallett changes a paper disc that records length of time the foghorn was in operation (1962).
(Photo: Falmouth Enterprise, April 17, 1962).

Controls

An electronic sensing control was installed in 1968 to automatically turn the fog signal on whenever fog rolled in. The device transmitted flashing light rays capable of sensing moisture density[71] in fog, heavy rain, or snow, and reflect its signal back to activate the foghorn.[72]

Assistant Nobska keeper Gary Williams, USCG, told reporters in 1983 that the dual foghorns recorded only sixty-five decibels from inside the keepers quarters and that this sound level is equivalent to the average human voices talking.[73]

---

[71] National Archives at Boston in Waltham, Massachusetts and Falmouth Enterprise, September 27, 1968.

[72] National Archives at Boston in Waltham, Massachusetts, notice to mariners no. 109.

[73] *Cape Cod Times*, February 13, 1983.

MRASS Electronic Fog-Signaling System

In December 2018, the obsolete fog-signaling equipment was replaced with a new state-of-the-art electronic system known as the "Mariner Radio Activated Sound Signal" (MRASS). The new system operates on a frequency of 157.175 MHz Channel 83A and is remotely activated by mariners at sea by simply keying their marine transmitter five consecutive times. Once the MRASS system activates, the fog signal sounds for up to one hour before automatically shutting down and returning to a standby mode. MRASS equipped lighthouse stations throughout the United States are noted on appropriate navigational charts.

As of 1968, the brick equipment building has been used to house the radio beacon equipment, fog-signaling equipment, emergency backup battery banks, the new MRASS fog-signaling equipment, as well as for USCG storage. However, the sound-producing horns are still located across the street from the Nobska Light Station on the bluff at Vineyard Sound, facing Martha's Vineyard Island.

The electronic MRASS System (2018).
(Photo by the author)

Radio Beacon

In 1937, a new 125-foot steel transmitter tower[74] was erected approximately seventy-five feet west of the light tower. The transmitter and electronic transmitting equipment for the radio beacon was located in the brick equipment building.

The Nobska radio beacon transmitter was one of three radio beacons in the area consisting of the Nobska Point Light Station, the Butler Flats Light Station in New Bedford, and the Cleveland Ledge Lighthouse[75] on Buzzards Bay. Each station transmitted a different letter in Morse code on a different frequency.

The Nobska station transmitted the letter G in Morse code – – · (dah-dah-dit) repeatedly for one minute every six minutes. The signals received from these three locations helped mariners to determine their "fix" at sea.

Relocate the Radio Beacon

In January 1948, a sixty-five-foot wooden transmitter mast was temporarily installed and wired to continue with transmissions while provisions were being made to relocate the 125-foot steel mast to its permanent location. The cement foundation for the mast was poured on July 12, 1948, approximately one hundred feet northeast of the light tower and directly behind the new equipment building.[76] Then on August 2, 1948, a hundred-foot crane boom was used to dismantle the mast in sections, then reassemble in its new location behind the equipment building.

---

[74] Massachusetts Historical Commission, 80 Boylston Street, Boston, Massachusetts, 02116, dated July 24, 1981, file 87001483.pdf and National Achieves at Boston Waltham, Massachusetts, letter, dated July 18, 1961.

[75] Falmouth Enterprise newspaper, September 27, 1968.
Cleveland Ledge Lighthouse was named for President Grover Cleveland's favorite fishing spot. The lighthouse replaced a lightship that had been there for many years.

[76] National Archives at Boston in Waltham, Massachusetts.

Keeper's logbook entry

June 12, 1948: The radio technician replaced an 807 RF transmitter vacuum tube. The 807 vacuum tube was very common transmitter tube. The high power beacon transmitter may have used several of these tubes.

New site of the 125-foot steel radio beacon
transmitter tower (August 1948).
The transmitting and fog-signaling equipment were
located inside the equipment building (*center*).

Twenty-four underground radial wires (ground plane) extending outward every fifteen degrees around the base of the transmitter mast were a necessary part of the installation.[77] The ID transmitted

---

[77] National Archives at Boston in Waltham, Massachusetts, drawing no. 5271, December 26, 1956.

from the radio beacon was later changed to Morse code letters NP for Nobska **P**oint – · · – – · (dah-dit, dit-dah-dah-dit). The cost of this move was $2,000.[78]

In 1961, the frequency of the Nobska radio beacon was changed from its original frequency[79] (frequency not documented) to 324 kilohertz.[80] The frequency was later changed to 292 kilohertz.[81]

Keeper Osborne Earl Hallett records the time the radio beacon signals were transmitted (1962).

---

[78] Massachusetts Historical Commission, 80 Boylston Street, Boston, Massachusetts, dated July 24, 1981, file 87001483.pdf. National Achieves at Boston in Waltham, Massachusetts, letter, dated July 18, 1961.

[79] Documentation on the frequency of the original beacon transmitter could not be located. However, research is ongoing, and information will be available in following editions of this book.

[80] Notice to mariners no. 47, November 13, 1961.

[81] Date not documented. However, a newspaper article, dated February 2, 1965, written by Edward Rowe Snow, explains the radio beacon transmitter frequency was 292 kilohertz.

Telephone

A telephone was installed in the equipment building in 1961 to provide communications between the Nobska keeper and the keeper at the West Chop Lighthouse on Martha's Vineyard Island.

Hand-cranked telephone in the equipment building (1961).
(Photo by the author)

CHAPTER 5

Historical Attractions Around Nobska

Martha's Vineyard (1602)

MARTHA'S VINEYARD ISLAND was discovered by English explorer Bartholomew Gosnold in 1602 and named after his daughter. The island is 26 miles long from Gay Head to Edgartown and located east of Vineyard Sound and 2.3 miles south off the coast of Woods Hole on Cape Cod, Massachusetts.

Woods Hole (1800s)

By the early 1800s, Woods Hole was the center of the whale trade. Nine whaling ships were docked in Great Harbor, supporting the local economy of chandlers, outfitters, candlemakers, and processors of whale oil and whalebone. Old captains' homes can be seen on many streets. Fishing, farming, whaling, local industries, summer playgrounds, events, and modern marine science are but a few of the attractions in Woods Hole. The annual world-famous "Falmouth race" starting line is right in the center of Woods Hole on Water Street.

Pacific Guano Works (1863)

Under the US Guano Act, the Pacific Guano Works claimed the Howland Islands at the equator in the Pacific in 1859 for their own use. They searched Cape Cod for the best spot for their factory and chose Woods Hole because of its natural deepwater harbor. They bought several acres of land on Penzance Point and built their first factory there in 1863.

Sulfur from Italy, nitrate of soda from Chile, potash from Germany, local hauls of menhaden fish, and phosphorus from South America and the Caribbean supplied a heavy demand from growers around the country. The need to transport thousands of tons of fertilizer brought the railroad to Woods Hole.

Ten vessels were used to bring bird droppings from South America, and fish parts collected from local fisheries, to the Pacific Guano fertilizer manufacturing plant.

Pacific Guano Works in 1863.

For whatever reasons, by 1889, the finances of the company were in ruin, and bankruptcy was declared. The buildings and dock were abandoned, and the Pacific Guano Works closed. Although history has now laid blame on its treasurer John Glidden, the factory more than doubled the population of Woods Hole during its twenty-six-year history.

Woods Hole Science Aquarium (1885)

The aquarium was established in 1885 in Woods Hole and is America's oldest marine aquarium for public education and scientific research.

Marine Biological Laboratory (MBL) (1888)

The world-renowned Marine Biological Laboratory was founded in Woods Hole in 1888. Since then, the MBL provided a home to well over half a hundred Nobel Prize laureates. An international center for research and education in biological and environmental science, the MBL is a private, nonprofit institution.

Woods Hole Oceanographic Institution (WHOI) (1930)

WHOI is the world's leading independent nonprofit organization dedicated to ocean research, exploration, and education. Scientists recognized the clear water in Woods Hole caused by strong currents, the perfect deep anchorages areas for research vessels, and the central location midway along the most heavily fished stretches of New England.

The Woods Hole Oceanographic Institution was created in 1930. Original captains' houses line the main streets in the village of Woods Hole. Scientists and engineers push the boundaries of knowledge about the ocean to reveal its impacts on our planet and our lives. The wreck of the *Titanic* was a discovery by WHOI on September 1, 1985, when one of *Titanic*'s boilers was identified and confirmed.

Discovery of the *Titanic* in 1985.

Geodesic Dome (1953)

About one mile north of Nobska Point Light is the oldest surviving Geodesic Dome in the world, constructed in 1953 by students under the guidance of designer and patent holder Buckminster Fuller. These students traveled from across the country to Woods Hole to build the Dome.

They precut the wooden members of the structure on the campus of MIT and transported them to the site, where the team lived for three weeks while erecting the structure. Built to serve as the restaurant for the Nautilus Motor Inn, the dome survived early criticism and operated successfully for decades. Over the years, the dome became a beloved fixture in the village, a destination for special dinners, and a highlight for tourists.

The Dome as it stands today.
(Photo by the author)

The dome fell out of use around 2002, and efforts to redevelop the property have not been successful. Sadly, the historic midcentury modern Nautilus Inn has been allowed to wither and decay and now beyond repair while the dome also suffers from roof leaks, animal intrusion, and vandalism.

Beginning in 2016, several different groups began looking at the dome. However, any effort to preserve this site must come with a plan for its future. A developer recently bought the five-acre property for nearly $3 million.

Bartholomew Gosnold

English explorer Bartholomew Gosnold sailed from Falmouth, England, and discovered the Elizabeth Islands and Martha's Vineyard Island in June 1602 on his way to Virginia eighteen years before the arrival of the Mayflower in Plymouth. All the Elizabeth Islands were originally given Native American names.

Gosnold built a fort and established a colony on Cuttyhunk Island, which only lasted several weeks because his crew ran out of supplies. Gosnold and his crew decided to return to England. In 1641, English colonialists claimed and settled on the islands as part of England's expansion.

They renamed the chain of islands after Queen Elizabeth. Thomas Mayhew of Watertown, Massachusetts, purchased the islands in the same year along with Nantucket Island and Martha's Vineyard Island. The islands were part of Dukes County, New York, before the creation of Massachusetts.

Elizabeth Islands

The Elizabeth Islands span for sixteen miles off the southwestern tip of Cape Cod, Massachusetts, and consists of twenty-two islands, which make up the town of Gosnold, Dukes County. The closest island to the mainland in Woods Hole is 1.4 miles, and the farthest is 15.4 miles. The town of Gosnold is the smallest of the 351 towns in Massachusetts and has a population of only thirty. The Gosnold town government and town hall is located in the town of Gosnold on Cuttyhunk Island.

The series of islands are located east of Buzzards Bay, and west of Vineyard Sound and can only be reached by boat or aircraft. The state of Massachusetts owns Penikese Island, and the town of Gosnold owns Cuttyhunk Island.

The Forbes Family Trust owns the remainder of the Elizabeth Islands. Regardless of where you live on the Elizabeth Islands, you live in Gosnold, Massachusetts.

Elizabeth Islands (Alphabetical Order)

Bachelor Island

Bachelor Island is a small barren rock just off the northeastern coast of Naushon Island and southwest of Monohansett Island.

Baret Island

Baret Island is a small sandy but mostly rocky oval-shaped island located just off the near midnorthern coast of Nashawena Island, northeast of Rock Island, southeast of a peninsula known as the "Neck" on Nashawena Island, and directly north of Middle Pond on Nashawena.

Bull Island

Bull Island is located between Nonamesset and Uncatena Islands and separates Hadley Harbor from Inner Harbor. Enjoy the wooded landscape, mixed rock and sand shoreline, and gorgeous harbor views visible on the trails around Bull Island. One of the best trails provides a 360-degree view of Hadley Harbor in less than a half hour of exploration. Walk the trail that starts from the small dock on the south side of the island and leads to its western edge, ending in a beautiful grove of birch trees that overlooks a small sandy beach.

This western point is a lovely place to view a sunset. Coyotes and foxes can be spotted here, both onshore and swimming between the islands. Bull Island is home to garter snakes as well as many insects and birds. The waters of Hadley Harbor are full of ocean life, including sea stars, whelks, crabs, and shellfish. Harbor seals can be seen in the winter.

Cedar Island

Cedar Island is located between Monohansett and Nonamesset Islands and 2.3 miles southwest of Woods Hole. The island is named due to the small cedar trees that grow on it.

Cuttyhunk Island

Cuttyhunk Island is the outermost island and was a small outpost for harvesting sassafras. It was the first English settlement in New England. It's located between Buzzards Bay and Vineyard Sound. Its name comes from a Wampanoag Indian term, meaning "a thing that lies out in the great water." The town hall for the town of Gosnold is in Gosnold, Cuttyhunk Island. It's the fourth largest island, and its population was seventy-five persons as of 2010. Cuttyhunk Island has a one-room schoolhouse with four current students. This island is known for its first-class fishing.

Gosnold Island

Gosnold Island is located in Westend Pond on Cuttyhunk Island. It was named for its founder, Bartholomew Gosnold.

Gull Island

Gull Island is a small uninhabited island located just off the southeast coast of Penikese Island and between Cedar and Naushon Islands. It was used as a bombing practice area for Navy aviators from 1941 to 1957.

Monohansett Island

Monohansett Island population was thirty persons as of 2000. The island is seven miles long.

Nashawena Island

Nashawena Island is three miles long and has grazing livestock. It is the second largest island and located east of Cuttyhunk Island and west of Pasque Island. The island has an official permanent population of two persons as of 2000. Nashawena is an Indian word, meaning "middle island."

Naushon Island

Naushon Island is the largest of the Elizabeth Islands with a population of thirty as of 2000 and is located seven miles from

Woods Hole. It is 5.5 miles long and is mainland to five smaller islands: Nonamesset Island, Monohansett Island, Bull Island, Cedar Island, and Bachelor Island. Naushon Island was a British naval base in 1812. Students on this island commute to the mainland to attend school.

The Forbes family has their own private ferry on this island, and several family members live on these islands year-round to care for their properties and farm animals. Although not generally open to the public, the Forbes family has set aside Tarpaulin Cove (south) and Kettle Cove (north), as well as Bull Island and Hadley Harbor to the northeast for picnicking and public enjoyment. Trucks, tractors, horses, cows, and sheep are allowed on Forbes's islands. However, cars are not allowed. Tarpaulin lighthouse is on this island.

Nonamesset Island

Nonamesset Island is the most easterly and closest island to mainland Woods Hole 1.4 miles. This island was uninhabited as of the 2000 census.

Pasque Island

Pasque Island is 1.5 miles long and 9.6 miles from Woods Hole. It is located between Nashawena Island to its west and Naushon Island to its east. The island is a shallow tidal creek that cuts partway through the island. The island is covered in poison ivy. The population is two persons as of 2000.

Penikese Island

Penikese Island is 13.9 miles from Woods Hole and one-half mile northwest of Cuttyhunk Island. Penikese Island was the site of a research facility in the 1800s, which brought fame to the Marine Biological Laboratory (MBL) in Woods Hole. From 1905 until 1921, this island was also home to the only leprosy hospital in Massachusetts.

This island is also home to the Penikese Island School established in 1973 as a private, independent, Massachusetts-accredited organization. The school is for troubled boys—an alternative to prison. It is also a bird sanctuary. The island is state-owned and publicly accessible.

Rock Island

Rock Island is located off the north shore of Nashawena Island and 2.3 miles east-northeast of Cuttyhunk.

Uncatena Island

Uncatena Island is the most northerly of the Elizabeth Islands and located just off the northernmost point of Naushon Island. Uncatena was uninhabited as of 2000.

Veckatimest Island

Veckatimest Island was uninhabited as of 2000.

Weepecket Islands

Weepecket Islands are a group of three small islands off the north shore of Naushon Island. They were used for US military bombing and machine gun practice, from 1941 to 1957. The islands are uninhabited and popular breeding ground for double-crested cormorants. They are home to shorebirds, seals, and other animals.

CHAPTER 6

Lighthouse Organization and Nobska Visitor Rules

Introduction

NOBSKA'S ORIGINAL LIGHTHOUSE was built when the US Lighthouse Establishment was in control of all lighthouses in the United States. This chapter explains other lighthouse organizations that came to power from the USLHE to the present Friends of Nobska Organization.

Organizations

US Lighthouse Establishment (1789)

The US Congress created the US Lighthouse Establishment (USLHE) in 1789 under the Treasury Department.

US Lighthouse Board (1851)

The US Lighthouse Board was created in 1851 by the US government and staffed by scientists and mariners who soon arranged to provide America's coastline with Fresnel lenses. In 1865, the US Lighthouse Board adopted the practice of naming its tenders after flowers, trees, or plants. In 1903, the US Lighthouse Board was transferred from the US Treasury Department to the Department of Commerce and Labor and, in 1910, was recognized as the Bureau of Lighthouses. However, Congress abolished the US Lighthouse Board in 1910 because its nine-member team was too cumbersome.

US Bureau of Lighthouses / US Lighthouse Service (1852–1910)

Between July 1, 1852, and 1910, Congress created the US Bureau of Lighthouses operated as the US Lighthouse Service (USLHS) under the control of the Department of Commerce and Transportation. The USLHS was expanded in 1930 to include aids to navigation (ATON) and lightships. Due to increasing costs to import Fresnel lenses from France, the USLHS encouraged glass factories in the United States to produce lighthouse lenses.

Regulations in 1835 did not allow hiring Negros upon lightships, except for cooks. Although the USLHS discriminated against Negros, they were present throughout the American history of lighthouses. However, there has been no evidence of Negros obtaining a keepers' position.

Little Harbor in Woods Hole, Massachusetts, was established as the repair and supply center for the USLHS in 1857.

US Lighthouse Service adopted a distinctive pennant flag in 1869, which was triangular in shape with a red border and blue lighthouse on a white background. The lighthouse vessels displayed this flag.

US Light House Service (USLHS) pennant flag.

In 1939, the US Congress terminated the Bureau of Lighthouses, and all activities were given to the USCG. Lighthouses were once again under the control of the US Treasury Department.

The 150th anniversary of the US Lighthouse Service was called for by a joint resolute on May 15, 1939, and signed by the president. By this resolution, the week of August 7 was designated "Lighthouse Week," celebrating the operation of the USLHE on August 7, 1789.

Bureau of Navigation (1884)

This organization was formed in 1884.

US Coast Guard Responsible for Nobska (1939)

The US Coast Guard replaced the Lighthouse Bureau on July 7, 1939. The USCG was responsible for the maintenance of all lighthouses in the United States. The USCG offered Nobska Light Station to municipalities in 2015 for nonprofit or for private sale.

Four organizations in Falmouth concerned with historic preservation banded together under the Town of Falmouth to form a new nonprofit to bid for the license and its 2.3 acres site. The Town of Falmouth was accepted in September 2015, and the parties entered into a licensing process, which was completed in 2016.

US Coast Guard Auxiliary (1939)

The US Coast Guard Auxiliary was established by Congress in 1939 as a uniformed volunteer component of USCG under the Department of Homeland Security. After Nobska Light was added to the National Historical Registry, maintenance of the lighthouse became the responsibility of the US Coast Guard Auxiliary.

National Historical Registry (1987)

On June 15, 1987, the Nobska Point Light Station was added to the National Historical Registry as Light no. 31, registration no. 87001483.

Friends of Nobska Light (2017)

Friends of Nobska Light is a nonprofit organization formed in 2017 by the Falmouth Historical Society, Highfield Hall and Gardens, Woods Hole Historical Museum, and the Woods Hole Community Association. The mission of Friends of Nobska Light is the preservation and protection of this beloved landmark to ensure its future enjoyment for the community and visitors.

The town handed over renovation and maintenance to the nonprofit Friends of Nobska Light. When restoration is complete, the Friends of Nobska Light will operate the lighthouse as a museum open to the public for free. Nobska will then join the hundred-plus lighthouses in the country that have passed from federal to local and private management since global positioning systems and other improvements to navigation reduced the need for manned lighthouses. The Friends of Nobska Light offer tours of the lightkeeper's house.

The light tower was opened for tours in the summer of 2017 and by late March 2017, the Friends of Nobska Light had raised roughly $66,000 but were planning to ask the Town to provide the approximately $265,000 still required to proceed with the restoration.

Voters approved allocating $264,000 in April 2016 toward the restoration of Nobska Lighthouse, and the US Coast Guard granted a license for the property to the Town of Falmouth.

Town of Falmouth

Town of Falmouth approved a license with the US Coast Guard in March 2016, which made the town the stewards of Nobska Light and responsible for maintaining the four-acre site, keepers' dwellings, and the light tower. Work was done by the Friends of Nobska Light.

Nobska Light and keepers' dwellings are now a museum and will be open to the public for free.

Phase 1: Restore lighthouse.
Phase 2: Restore dwellings and convert to museums.

Nobska Visitor Restrictions

Public Events Permitted on the Grounds at Nobska Light

1. Maximum of two hours on the property for any event.
2. Christmas by the sea caroling (Santa by helicopter).
3. Weddings.
4. Wedding photographs.
5. Marriage engagements.
6. Birthday parties.
7. Family reunions.
8. Family portraits.
9. Tour requests.
10. Newspaper or TV interviews.

Nobska Visitor Admissions, Rules, and Restrictions

1. Children must be at least six years of age and forty-five inches tall to enter the lighthouse.
2. Shoes and shirts are required anywhere inside the museum or inside the lighthouse.
3. Food or drinks are not permitted inside the museum or lighthouse.
4. Smoking is not permitted inside the lighthouse or buildings.
5. Backpacks, large purses, or large camera bags are not allowed in the lightroom.
6. Infants in carrying pouches are not allowed in the lightroom.

7. Liability is not accepted for personal items left unattended on Nobska property.
8. Tents shall not be placed on Nobska property. Use of restrooms is not allowed.
9. Chairs are not allowed on Nobska property.
10. Specific times, dates, and the number of visitors to attend Nobska lighthouse are required.
11. Tour guides cannot accept monetary donations or gifts for conducting tours.

CHAPTER 7

Interesting Facts

Fresnel Lens

FRESNEL LENSES CONVERT its internal light source, such as an oil lamp or electric light bulb, by means of reflection and refraction through prisms into a bright and powerful horizontal light beam. The beam helps mariners at sea to determine their location, guides them to avoid sailing into hazardous waters, and provides a safe passage through dangerous areas.

The present Nobska fourth-order Fresnel lens is presently valued at around $250,000, whereby a first-order lens is presently valued at around $2,000,000. These lenses are cleaned with a cloth and a mixture of distilled water, alcohol, and Woolite.

Where Is the Most Powerful Fresnel Lens in the World?

Makalu's lighthouse on Oahu's most southeastern point of Hawaii uses the world's largest hyper-radiant lens. The inside diameter of the lens is over 8 feet, the tower is approximately 45 feet tall, and the focal plane is 425 feet.

How Many Lighthouses in the World?

About 18,900.

Which Country Has the Most Lighthouses?

The United States has more lighthouses than any other country in the world.

Which State Has the Most Lighthouses?

Michigan with 118. New York is next with 80.

Lighthouse Types

There are many styles of lighthouses found around the globe. Many were used as dwellings with the keepers' families living in them. Those built in deep water were reached by boat with a ladder or steps to climb into the lighthouse.

At some lighthouses, an entire boat and its passengers were hoisted up to the living areas of the lighthouse. Boats were hung on divots until needed.

Skeletal-Frame-Type Lighthouse

Often referred to as pyramidal-type lighthouses. The metal skeletal-frame lighthouses on land were designed for low wind resistance and to allow seawater to wash under them without damage to the lighthouse. People did not normally live in such lighthouses. The only skeletal-frame lighthouse in New England is in Marblehead, Massachusetts.

Conical-Type Lighthouse

Conical lighthouses are similar to "round" lighthouses. However, if the light tower at the top is narrower than the bottom, it's classified as a conical. Keepers typically passed through a small building or entrance room that is connected to or separate from the dwelling to access the tower, then climb a spiral stairway to the lightroom.

Conical-type lighthouse (Rebuilt Nobska Light).

Screw-Pile-Type Lighthouse

Forty-two screw-pile lighthouses were built on the Chesapeake Bay between 1850 and 1900—more than anywhere in the world. The screw-pile lighthouse was developed by Alexander Mitchell, who was a blind Irish marine engineer. Iron legs were screwed into the bed at the bottom of the water usually in a hexagonal pattern. A one-and-a-half-story cottage for the keeper was built on top of this foundation, and a light was placed on top of the cottage. The legs of the foundation were protected from ice with piles of stones. Screw piles were usually built on shoals or at the mouth of a river.

Caisson-Type Lighthouse

A caisson is a cast-iron cylinder sunk deep into the bottom of the waterbed and filled with heavy stones and concrete. The tower of iron or brick was then built on top of the caisson foundation. Resembles an automobile spark plug.

A caisson-type lighthouse looks like a spark plug.

The first caisson lighthouse erected in the United States was the *Craighill Channel Lower Range Front Light*. Caisson lighthouses were expensive to build but very sturdy.

Stag Lighthouse

This is not a "type" of lighthouse but rather an isolated lighthouse located in a remote area surrounded by water and not attached by land. Stag lighthouses are operated solely by single men and not suitable as a residence for families, thus, the name "stag." Living at a stag lighthouse meant food and supplies had to be delivered via boat.

Integral-Type Lighthouse

An integral lighthouse is a house with a light on top. Building an integral lighthouse is simple and no more expensive than building a house. The original Nobska lighthouse was an example of an integral lighthouse.

Integral-type lighthouse (Original Nobska Light).

Many early lighthouses were of this type. From 1852 to 1853, there was a movement to replace integral lights that were in poor condition with much taller tower-type lighthouses.

Texas Tower-Type Lighthouse

Texas Tower-type lighthouses were modeled upon offshore oil drilling rigs typical of those off the Texas coast. They are made of steel.

Schoolhouse-Type Lighthouses

This style lighthouse was constructed similar to an old school-house, hence the name. The house is typically all brick with an integrated tower built into the keepers' dwelling. This was a common style. Others were designed using wood. It was a simple design and cost-effective for harbor lights.

Lightship Type

During 1930, lightships were not self-propelled. Instead, they were towed out to their stations and left with a crew. Baskets were often woven to alleviate boredom.

How Many Lighthouses When We Became a Nation in 1776?

Twelve.

Where Is the Highest Lighthouse Above Sea Level in America?

Dillon Reservoir Lighthouse in Frisco, Colorado, is 9,017 feet above sea level.

Where Can I View Multiple Lighthouses?

From Nobska Light Station in Woods Hole, Massachusetts:

1. East Chop Light
2. West Chop Light
3. Gay Head Light
4. Tarpaulin Cove Light
5. Pogue Light

From Portland Head Light in Cape Elizabeth, Maine:

1. Halfway Rock Light
2. Seguin Light
3. Ram Island Ledge Light
4. Spring Point Ledge Light
5. Cape Elizabeth Lights
6. Cape Elizabeth Lights

From Avery Point Light in Groton, Connecticut:

1. New London Harbor Light
2. New London Ledge Light
3. Little Gull Island Light
4. Race Rock Light

Oldest Wooden Lighthouse in America!

Poplar Point light in North Kingston, Rhode Island (now privately owned).

Where Was the First Fog Signal in America?

The first fog signal in the United States was a cannon, which was installed at America's first light station in Boston, Massachusetts, on Little Brewster Island in 1716.

Vessels entering Boston Harbor fired a cannon, and the keeper would respond by firing its cannon. This gave the mariner a fairly good idea of the direction of the Boston Lighthouse and the entrance to Boston Harbor.

Ten Oldest Lighthouses in America

	Year	*State*	*Rebuilt*	*Name*
1.	1716	Massachusetts	1783	Boston Light
2.	1746	Massachusetts	1901	Brant Point Light
3.	1749	Rhode Island	1856	Beavertail Light
4.	1760	Connecticut	1801	New London Light
5.	1764	New Jersey	Original	Sandy Hook Light
6.	1768	Massachusetts	1843	Plymouth Light
7.	1785	Massachusetts	1986	Great Point Light
8.	1788	Massachusetts	1898	Newburyport Light
9.	1791	Maine	Original	Portland Head Light
10.	1791	Massachusetts	1820	Bakers Island Light

Three Oldest Lighthouses in the World

1. 280 BC   Pharos Island at   Not Standing
               Alexandria, Egypt
2. 61 BC   Tower of Hercules, La   Still Standing
               Coruña Galicia, Spain
3. AD 40   Roman lighthouse,   Still Standing
               Dover, England

Tower of Hercules,
La Coruña
61 BC
Galicia, Spain.
(Satellite photo by author)

Roman Lighthouse
AD 40
Dover, England.
(Plan view satellite photo by author)

People Who Study Lighthouses

People who study lighthouses are called "pharologists." The name comes from the famous world's first lighthouse in Alexandria, Egypt, built around 300–270 BC.

Dimensional Chart for Fresnel Lenses (Approximations)

Fresnel Order	Height	Inside Diameter	Weight Pounds	Weight Approximate 1851 costs
First	10'10"	7'0"	12,800	$6,800
Second	6'1"	4'7"	3,527	4,400
Third	4'8"	3'3"	1,948	1,860
Fourth (Nobska)	2'4"	1'8"	600	1,250
Fifth	2'0"	1'0"	300	Unknown
Sixth	1'0"	0'11"	145	Unknown

Prior to 1789 lighthouses were built and controlled by local municipalities resulting in a lack of uniformity in their operation. However, after George Washington became president, the Lighthouse Act was established on August 7, 1789. Then in 1791, all lighthouses in the United States were under the control of the US federal government. The president ordered all lighthouses to be maintained at all times by a keeper living on site.

Oil Consumption Chart for Fresnel Lenses with Oil Lamps[82] (Approximations)

Fresnel Lens order	Wickes Used	Ounces of Oil Per Hour	Ounces Oil Per 12 Hour (avg)	Daily Gallons of Oil	Weekly Gallons of Oil	Annual Gallons of Oil
First	4	26.3	316	3.00	21.00	1,092
Second	3	17.5	210	2.00	14.00	728
Third	2	07.0	84	0.80	5.60	291
Fourth (Nobska)	2	05.3	64	0.61	4.27	222
Fifth (Nobska)	1	03.2	38	0.36	2.52	131

Early Lighthouse Keepers

Lighthouses built in the 1700s, such as in Massachusetts from 1716 to 1784, were provided with local male keepers from municipalities in which the lighthouse was built.

Lighthouse Markings

Markings on lighthouses are called "daymarks." It was determined by the Lighthouse Board in the early 1900s that land built lighthouses should have distinctive markings against backgrounds so that mariners can easily identify them by day.

---

[82] Based on kerosene weight of 15.33 fluid ounces per pound, 6.82 pounds per gallon, and 183 fifteen-hour winter nights, and 183 eight-hour summer nights.
18 fluid ounces = 1 pound
6.9 pounds = 1gallon

CHAPTER 8

Fresnel Lens

Augustin Jean Fresnel

THE FRENCH PHYSICIST and engineer Augustin Fresnel designed a lens in 1819 for use in lighthouses to increase visibility distance, reduce maintenance time and maintenance costs. Fresnel lenses named after its inventor were good indefinitely with minimal maintenance required. These lenses quickly became in great demand and replaced conventional lighting systems consisting of multiple lamps and reflectors. Fresnel lenses became the standard optic for all lighthouses worldwide.

(May 10, 1788 to July 14, 1827)
Augustin Jean Fresnel at age thirty-seven,
only two years before his death.

Part 1: Principles of the Fresnel Lens

Introduction

Fresnel lens

The larger the lens, the more prism rings will be employed, and hence, the higher the intensity and further away the light can be seen from the sea and through poor weather conditions. The focal plane of the light also determines the distance the light can be seen. The higher the light, the further it can be seen. However, earth's horizon is always the limiting factor.

Magnifying Glass Example

The typical magnifying glass will be used to help explain the concept of the Fresnel lens (see photo). When light enters the flat surface of a magnifying glass, refraction (bending of the light) occurs at the curvature (arc) surface of the glass. All the outgoing light is concentrated into an intense narrow beam.

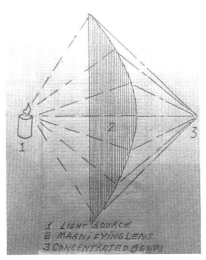

Typical magnifying glass.
(Sketch by the author)

A high percentage of light is absorbed in the thickness of a magnifying glass, which significantly reduces its ability to efficiently refract light waves. If we could remove the useless sections from our magnifying glass, we would dramatically reduce the weight of the lens, reduce the size, reduce the cost, and increase the efficiency of the lens to refract maximum light.

Suppose our magnifying glass were made of a material that could easily be removed. We could cut away the four clear vertical useless parts of the glass and leave behind the nine useful outer shaded areas (see photo).

Shaded areas are useful parts of the lens.
(Sketch by the author)

Observe the four equally spaced vertical lines through the glass and where each line intersects with the upper and lower curvatures of the glass. The useful parts of the glass that we want to keep are the shaded areas. Save those shaded areas and remove the remaining "clear" areas of the glass, as they are rendered useless (see photo).

Position the shaded areas onto the flat surface of the glass. The glass now becomes a Fresnel lens. The shaded parts are the prisms, which refract the light horizontally and outward (see photo).

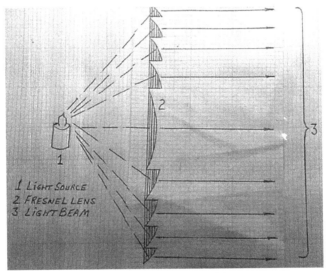

End product...a Fresnel lens!
(Sketch by the author)

Part 2: How Does the Fresnel Lens Work?

Introduction

Light is similar to sound, in that it travels in all directions, up/down, front/back, left/right. With the Fresnel lens removed from its assembly and only its internal light source remaining, light waves would still travel in all directions but dim and very difficult to be seen from any great distance.

There is a bull's-eye lens in the center of each segment of the lens and prism rings encircling the internal light source. There is a space between each prism ring.

Range of the Light

The luminous range of a Fresnel lens is determined by the intensity of its light source and by the radius distance from the light source to the inside of the lens, referred to as the *focal distance or focal length*. Fresnel lenses were designed to provide power levels from first order, being the most powerful, to the sixth order, being the least powerful. Nobska's forth order lens at its focal plane of eighty-seven feet is visible from approximately eleven nautical miles[83] from out at sea. However, visible distance of any light beam is limited by poor visible conditions and by the horizon at earths' curvature.

How the Powerful Light Is Created

The 250-watt bulb inside Nobska lens scatters its light waves through the center "bulls eye" of the lens, as well as striking the upper and lower prism rings.

Bull's-Eye

Light waves traveling straight through the center of the bull's-eye develops an outgoing intense horizontal beam.

Prisms above the Bull's-Eye

Light waves traveling upward strike all the prisms above the bull's-eye, which refracts the light to an outgoing intense horizontal beam.

---

[83] For formulas and more information on viewing distances, refer to Chapter 9.

Prisms below the Bull's-Eye

Light waves traveling downward strike all the prisms below the bull's-eye, which refracts the light to an outgoing intense horizontal beam.

Analogy

The analogy I often use to explain the operation of a Fresnel lens can be found in common "everyday" use, such as when calling to someone at a far distance you would typically use your hands to "cup" your mouth to project your voice. The sound waves guided by your "parabolic" shaped hands concentrate and reflect your voice to one direction, thus amplifying your sound.

Bull's-eye are in the center of each panel, with
prisms above and below the bull's-eye.
(Photo by the author)

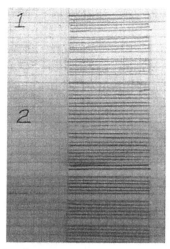

Looking into the Nobska lens
1. Prism rows.
2. Center bull's-eye.
(Sketch, authors' concept)

The height dimension of the combined upper, center, and lower outgoing beams is equal to the height dimension of the Fresnel lens. Despite the theoretical pattern of the outgoing beams, mariners out to sea will see only one bright light.

CHAPTER 9

Distance, Navigation, Nautical Miles

Introduction

IT IS MISLEADING when stating that a lighthouse with a hundred-foot focal plane, for example, claims its light can be seen for twenty-six miles out at sea. The maximum distance we can hope to see across sea level is to the horizon. Further is limited by the curvature of the earth. However, to see further, we must position ourselves higher above sea level. How much higher? How much further? When determining lighthouse distances, we need to understand that the distance from the light to the horizon is equal to the distance from the horizon to the light. To increase the distance from either direction, we must either increase the height of the focal plane or increase the height of the object at the horizon, such as the crow's nest on a vessel.

Part 1 (Viewing Distance)

How Far Can We See?

Geographical Range

A geographical range is the calculated maximum distance an object can be seen over water and is determined by its height.

Luminous Range

Luminous range is the maximum distance a light can travel and still be seen from over water. Luminous range is determined by its level of brightness. However, the earth's horizon is always the limiting factor.

One of the calculations to find the geographical range in nautical miles is rather simple. Multiply the square root of the height of an object by the constant 1.23.

For example, to find the luminous range of a light with a hundred-foot focal plane, simply multiply the square root of its height (10.0) by 1.23, and the distance will be 12.3 nautical miles.

Formula

Distance = ($\sqrt{\text{height of the light above sea-level in feet}}$) (1.23)

Distance = ($\sqrt{100 \text{ feet}}$) (1.23)

Distance = (10.0) (1.23)

Distance = 12.3 Nautical miles (14.2 Statute miles)

Exercise

Calculate the distance from Nobska's 87-foot focal plane.

Distance = ($\sqrt{\text{height of the light above sea-level in feet}}$) (1.23)

Distance = ($\sqrt{87 \text{ feet}}$) (1.23)

Distance = (9.3) (1.23)

Distance = 11.5 Nautical miles (13.2 Statute miles)

The height and brightness of a light determine the distance a light can be seen during clear conditions.

Distance from Object to Lighthouse

To find the distance from the height of any object to a lighthouse across open water,

1. calculate the distance from the height of the vessel to the horizon as explained above;
2. calculate the distance from the lighthouse to horizon as explained above; and
3. add both individual distances to arrive at the total distance from the vessel to the lighthouse.

Example

With Nobska's focal plane of 87 feet, its light can be seen from a vessel at 11.5 nautical miles away. Suppose the vessel was fitted with a 50-foot crow's nest. The maximum distance the vessel could see to the horizon would be 8.70 nm. Adding the two distances together gives the total distance of 19.28 nautical miles between the crow's nest and the lighthouse.

Distance from lighthouse to horizon	11.50 nm
Distance from vessel to horizon	08.70 nm
Distance between vessel and lighthouse	**20.20 nm**

Looming of Light

There's another factor that should be considered: looming of light.

Looming of light is an effect of refraction, or bending of light, due to atmospheric conditions. Because of looming, an observer may see the light slightly further than the above formulas reveal. Therefore, the constant of 1.32 may be used rather than 1.23. (The author prefers to use 1.23 as it automatically provides a safety margin.)

To obtain nautical miles, *divide* statute miles by 1.15.

To obtain statute miles, *multiply* nautical miles by 1.15.

To find the focal plane of a lighthouse when its distance in nautical miles is known:

Focal distance = $(D/1.23)^2$

Height versus Distance Chart (Approximations)

During clear weather conditions, the light from a lighthouse can be seen at various distances as indicated on the chart below, assuming the power of the optic is sufficient. The first column shows the lighthouse focal planes, the second column shows distances from lighthouse to horizon, the third column shows the distance from a 50-foot crow's nest to the horizon, and the fourth column shows the combined distance.

Lighthouse Focal Plane (Feet)	Distance from Lighthouse to Horizon (Nautical Mile)		Distance from 50-Foot High Crow's nest to Horizon (Nautical Mile)		Total Distance (Nautical Mile)
10	3.9	+	8.7	=	12.6
30	6.7	+	8.7	=	15.4
50	8.7	+	8.7	=	17.4
70	10.3	+	8.7	=	19.0
87 (Nobska)	11.5	+	8.7	=	20.2
90	11.7	+	8.7	=	20.4
110	12.9	+	8.7	=	21.6
130	14.0	+	8.7	=	22.7
150	15.1	+	8.7	=	23.8
170	16.0	+	8.7	=	24.7
190	17.0	+	8.7	=	25.7
210	17.8	+	8.7	=	26.5

Part 2: Navigation

Navigating a Course

In addition to navigational information, charts provide safety information about conditions on and under the water. The aid to navigation (ATON) is road markers in water, showing safe courses to pass other vessels. Charts provide guidance to navigation between red and green buoys in dangerous waters as they mark the deep safe water passages. Charted blue areas indicate depths less than 30 feet while white areas indicate deeper water. Water depths in Vineyard Sound are typically 120 feet but only 3 to 8 feet deep on other Island shoals. At one location several miles off Woods Hole, water depth is only 18 inches at low tide. Areas of charts projecting from a lighthouse and outlined in red are known as a red sector and mark bearings, where there are dangerous shoals, rocks, or shallow areas.

Mercator Projection Chart

A Mercator projection chart is a cylindrical chart in which longitudinal lines from the equator to the poles are arranged parallel with one another rather than converging at the poles, typical of other types of charts. Areas approaching the poles are intentionally made disproportionately larger to accommodate the parallel lines.

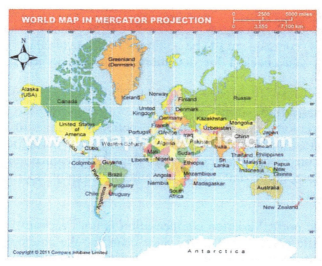

Mercator projection chart.

All lateral and longitudinal lines cross at right angles to facilitate simplicity in navigating and in measuring distances.

True North versus Magnetic North

True north is the location or point where the earth's north longitude lines converge at the North Pole. Magnetic north is the location or point where the earth's north magnetic fields converge near the North Pole. The difference is referred to as variation. Both true and magnetic north are displayed on navigational charts inside the compass rose.

Compass Rose

You may find the compass rose displayed in several areas on a chart depending on the chart scale, for convenience to the navigator. The compass rose is mainly used when plotting navigational courses.

The outer circle of the compass rose displays "true north" while the inner circle displays "magnetic north." Both circles are calibrated in degrees.

The amount of variation (distance between true and magnetic north) is indicated in degrees in the compass rose along with the chart's revision date. The compass rose is used in conjunction with moveable "parallel bars" to establish course bearings on charts.

Deviation

Deviation is compass error due to close by metallic objects. The ship's compass must be calibrated to compensate for metallic objects and in accordance with USCG guidelines. The compass must be checked for deviation before navigating.

Variation

Variation is due to nature's periodic change of the earth's magnetic field location relative to earth's fixed true north location and is stipulated on navigational charts as the difference in degrees between true north and magnetic north (currently approximately fifteen degrees west).

To sail true north, variation compensation is not necessary. However, to sail magnetic north, refer to the latest chart for the amount of variation degrees east or west, that must be compensated on the ship's compass.

Part 3: Nautical Miles versus Statute Miles

Definition/Conversion

Nautical miles are distances measured over water while statute miles are distances measured over land. Nautical miles vs. statute miles (1 nautical mile = 1.15 statute mile).

Why Use Nautical Miles?

Why are nautical miles used on navigational charts instead of statute miles? The short answer is "for simplicity." Using nautical miles makes calculating mileage distance for navigational purposes easy. However, using 60 miles per lateral degree works perfectly since sixty is based on a standard universal clock system of 60 seconds equal one minute and 60 minutes equals one hour. Now since the equator is 0° and the poles are each 90° from the equator, using 69 statute miles would be cumbersome, especially when dealing with minutes of a degree (') or seconds of a degree (").

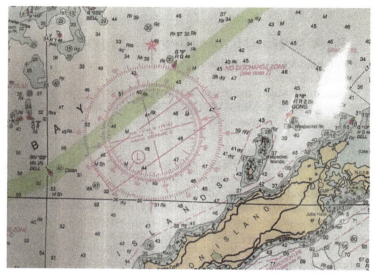

The compass rose (red circles). The 0° on the outer scale points to true north. The 0° on the inner scale points to magnetic north.
(Photo by the author)

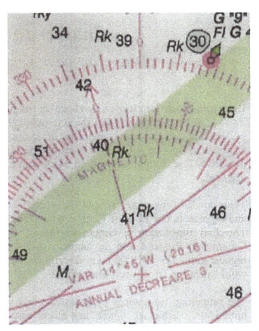

A close-up of a compass rose showing that in 2016 the difference (variation) between true north, outer scale, and magnetic north, inner scale was 14° 45' W.
(Photo by the author)

CHAPTER 10

Determine your Longitude

Determine Your Longitude Anywhere on the Planet

ON NOVEMBER 1, 1884, the international meridian confer-
ence held in Washington, DC, by a majority of nations decided on
Greenwich, England, as the location for the prime meridian, the 0°
longitude and an imaginary line from North Pole to South Pole passing through Greenwich, England.

There are twenty-four time zones around our planet. Each time
zone is 15° wide and represents one hour of earth rotation (360°/24
hours = 15° per hour). The first time zone is Greenwich Mean Time
(GMT) and starts in Greenwich, England. On an annual average in
Greenwich, the sun is highest in the sky at twelve noon directly above
the 0° longitude, hence, the word "mean" in Greenwich Mean Time.

The remaining time zones progress westerly every 15° from GMT
until 180° is achieved "where east meets west" at the *International
Date Line* exactly opposite Greenwich, England. Time zones continue westerly to a full circle at 360° or 0° Greenwich, England.

The 0° longitude in Greenwich, England, facing south.
Left foot in eastern hemisphere, right foot
in western hemisphere (2019).
(Photo by the author)

Although other countries cities, or areas, may be included in GMT, solar noon only occurs at twelve noon at 0° longitude. The *key* to finding your degree of longitude anywhere on the planet is to reference your exact *solar hour* to GMT either by calculating the time difference or by observing your watch set to GMT.

Reading Your GMT Watch

Regardless of where you are standing on the planet, your shadow will be shortest at the exact time the sun transits from east to west or when the sun is directly overhead. This time will represent your exact *solar noon.* At this moment, observe your GMT watch. Record hours and convert minutes to hours (minutes/60). Now multiply the GMT by 15° to obtain your degree of longitude.

Example

Suppose your GMT watch read 5:10 at the exact time of your solar noon. Convert the 10 minutes to a fraction of an hour (10/60 = 0.167 hours) then multiply 5.167 hours by 15° to obtain your longitude of 77.5° west.

A Word About Time Zones

Don't confuse longitudinal lines with time zones. Longitudinal lines are a function of solar noon exactly 15° apart while time zones are not. Each time zone covers an approximately three-hour period of 15° apart. However, for many reasons, times zones cannot be evenly spaced. In some locations, for example, time zones are configured to include islands, certain areas, and cities for the convenience of timekeeping. In fact, several time zones are only fifteen, thirty, or forty-five minutes apart, thereby, increasing the total number of times zones to more than twenty-four.

Nobska Time Line at a Glance

Year 1770: Winslow Lewis was born.
Year 1777: Smallpox inoculation hospital built in Falmouth Heights.
Year 1789: Government installing more lighthouses.
Year 1798: Smallpox inoculation hospital built on Nobska Point.
Year 1810: Winslow Lewis patent no. 1305 for lens/lamp/reflector system.
Year 1812: Lewis light test at Boston Light. Lewis patent sold to government included lamp installations.
Year 1829: Original Nobska built using ten Lewis lamps. Focal plane at eighty feet.

Year 1839: Lantern height extended to sixteen feet. Increased focal plane to ninety-six feet.

Year 1849: Lantern height extended to 24 feet. Increased focal plane to 104 feet.

Year 1850: Winslow Lewis died.

Year 1851: US Lighthouse Board established.

Year 1856: Fifth-order lens using one lamp replaced ten-Lewis-lamp system.

Year 1875: Removed original lighthouse. First Nobska fog bell installed.

Year 1876: Nobska Light rebuilt using same fifth-order lens and lamp. Focal plane at eighty-seven feet. Built new keepers' dwelling.

Year 1884: Keeper uniforms mandated by the US Lighthouse Board.

Year 1888: Forth-order lens replaced the fifth-order lens. Red sector added. Installed new machinery for the fog bell.

Year 1892: Seawall built to protect fog-signaling house.

Year 1899: Covered walkway installed.

Year 1900: New house for the fog machinery.

Year 1901: Brick oil house replaced the wooden oil house.

Year 1905: Assistants' dwelling added.

Year 1907: Modern fog bell tower replaced old fog bell tower.

Year 1911: Steam-compressed air whistle replaced the fog bell (bell used for standby).

TBD Steam-compressed air fog trumpet reed replaced fog whistle.

Year 1913: February. Light tower painted white for the first time.

Year 1914: IOV (incandescent oil vapor) lamp replaced the Argand lamp.

Year 1916: Medical benefits for keepers.

Year 1918: June 10. Removed fog bell house and machinery.

Built pigpen.

Year 1919: January 7. Electricity installed. The 150-watt bulb was used. Hencoop built.

May 10. Removed the modern fog bell tower.

Year 1935: Gas generator installed.

Year 1937: A 125-foot radio beacon installed.

Year 1938: Electric compressed air reed replaced the trumpet reed.

Year 1939: USCG Auxiliary established.

Year 1945: March 29. Built new brick building for fog signal and equipment.

Year 1948: August. Built brick equipment building. Relocated radio beacon tower.

Year 1949: December 6. Flagpole installed.

Year 1950: Two position lamp changer added using two 150-watt bulbs.

Year 1955: Seawall built to protect the road.

Year 1957: Oil furnace replaced coal in both dwellings.

Year 1959: June 6. A 1,000-watt bulb replaced the 150-watt bulb.

Year 1960: Floodlights installed to illuminate tower.

Year 1961: Telephone installed.

Year 1966: Vinyl siding replaced cedar shingles on both dwellings.

Year 1968: September. Storm flags displayed and lit by floodlights.

Year 1973: Last civilian keeper. First USCG keeper.

Year 1985: Light station automated to automatically operate the light and fog signal. First USCG resident. US Lighthouse Service established.

Year 1987: June 15. Nobska was added to the National Historical Registry as light no. 31, registration no. 87001483.

Year 2000: A 250-watt bulb replaced the 1000-watt bulb.

Year 2016: March. Town of Falmouth responsible for Nobska property, including dwellings and tower.

Year 2017: Friends of Nobska established.

Year 2018: MRASS automatic remote-controlled fog-signaling system installed.

GLOSSARY

Acetylene: A fuel used in some lighthouses after 1910. It was the first fuel to eliminate the need for a keeper to carry oil up the tower since it could be stored on the ground with an automatic sun detecting valve to turn the light off at daybreak and on again at dusk.

Aero beacon: A searchlight-type light originally designed for use at airports and adapted for use in a number of lighthouses.

Aid to navigation (ATON): A buoy, beacon, lighthouse, lightship, or any other structure or device built for the purpose of assisting navigation for vessels.

Arc of visibility: The portion of the horizon over which a lighted aid to navigation is visible from seaward.

Argand lamp: A hollow cylindrical wick oil lamp named after Ami Argand, the Swiss inventor who developed the design.

Astragal: Metal bar, running vertically or diagonally, used to frame and secure glass storm window panes of a lantern into sections.

ATON: An acronym for aid to navigation.

Beacon: A lighted aid to navigation.

Breakwater: A fixed or floating structure that protects shore areas, harbors, anchorage locations, or basin by breaking destructive, and powerful waves.

Bug light: Usually a very small tower.

Bull's-eye: Convex lens used to refract (concentrate) light.

Caisson-type lighthouse: Lighthouse built on an iron caisson. A caisson was essentially a hollow tube made of heavy rolled iron plates. The caissons were bolted together on land, transported into place, sunk and filled with sand, gravel, rock, or cement. Some referred to them as coffeepot lights or bug lights. After the invention of the internal combustion engine using spark plugs, caisson-type lighthouses became known as spark plug lights.

Candlepower: The brightness of a lighthouse is often expressed by its candlepower, where the amount of light produced is compared to how many candles it would take to achieve the same level of brightness.

Candlelight: An enclosed with candle optics. The first candlelit lighthouse had twenty-four candles.

Catwalk: A narrow elevated walkway, allowing the keeper access to light towers built out in the water. Synonymous with parapet.

Characteristics: The time interval and light pattern of a lighthouse. Nobska *flashes* once every *six* seconds.

Clockworks: The mechanism that revolved the light in early lighthouses. They were made up of gears, pulleys, and weights, which had to be manually wound by chains similar to winding a cuckoo clock. Clockworks had to be wound every four to six hours by the keeper. Large and heavy lenses were on rails and a platform floating in mercury, which performed the function of bearings. This concept allowed the light produced by an oil lamp to appear rotating. Clockworks became obsolete with the advent of electricity and its inherent ability to flash an electric light bulb.

Commissioned: The action of placing a previously discontinued aid to navigation back in operation.

Composite group flashing light: A group-flashing light in which the flashes combined in successive groups of different numbers of flashes.

Composite group occulting light: A light similar to a group-flashing light, except that the successive groups in a period have different numbers of eclipses.

Cottage-type lighthouse: A lighthouse comprised of a small one-story building that housed the keeper(s) with a light on top of the roof.

Crib: A structure, usually of timbers, that was sunk in water through filling with stone and served as the foundation for a concrete pier built atop it.

Daymark: Color scheme and pattern of lighthouses for identification during daylight hours.

Deviation: Compass error due to surrounding metallic ferrous objects.

Double-walled light tower: Light tower construction using an interior wall, as well as an exterior wall, to allow for taller and sturdy structures.

Eclipsing light: See occultation.

Emergency light: A light of reduced intensity displayed by certain aids to navigation when the main light is extinguished. The Nobska beacon on the parapet railing is an emergency beacon.

Fixed light: A continuous steady beam of light as opposed to a flashing light.

Flashing light: A light in which the total duration of light in each period is clearly shorter than the total duration of darkness and in which the flashes of light are all of equal duration. (Commonly used for a single-flashing light, which exhibits only single flashes repeated at regular intervals.) Nobska light flashes once every six seconds. Neighboring lighthouses have different characteristics so mariners can identify them on navigational charts. Opposite of osculating light.

Focal height: Synonymous with focal plane.

Focal length: Distance (radius) from the internal light source to the inside of a Fresnel lens. The longer the radius, the bigger the lens.

Focal plane: The distance from sea level at mean high tide (MHT) to the center of the lighthouse beam. Nobska's focal plane is eighty-seven feet.

Fog signal: An audible device to help mariners safely navigate during foggy or poor visibility conditions when light from a lighthouse is reduced. Bells, whistles, and horns, either manually or power-operated, were all used with varying degrees of success.

Fresnel, Agustin: French physicist Agustin Fresnel (Fra-nel) invented his Fresnel lens in 1822.

Fresnel lens (Fra-nel): A type of optic consisting of a convex lens and many prisms of glass used to intensify its internal light source through reflection and refraction. Named after its inventor Agustin Fresnel.

Fuel: A liquid or solid material burned to produce light in a lighthouse. Wood, whale oil, and kerosene are among many examples.

Geographic range: The range (distance) covered by a lighthouse increases with the height of the lighthouse. See luminous range.

Hyper radiant lens: Hyper-radiant lenses are Fresnel lenses used in lighthouses, which are larger than a first order lens.

Incandescent: An incandescent light bulb is an electric light with a wire filament heated to a high temperature that provides the light. The filament is protected from oxidation by an enclosed glass envelope filled with inert gas or vacuum.

Incandescent Oil Vapor Lamp (IOV): A type of lamp in which oil was hand pumped into a vaporizing chamber and then into a mantle. Similar to lamps used today for camping.

Inclination: Synonymous with variation.

Keeper: A person who operates and cares for a lighthouse or light-station.

Kerosene: A fuel commonly used in lighthouse oil lamps to provide the burning light source. Used after the use of whale oil.

Lamp: The light source typically in front of a polished reflector or inside a Fresnel lens.

Lantern: The entire glass enclosure at the top of a lighthouse that houses and protects the lightroom optic. The parapet is part of the lantern.

Lens: Curved glass or plastic device used in conjunction with a light source to spread and concentrate light from its source to an outgoing powerful horizontal beam.

Lewis lamp: An oil lamp similar to an Argand lamp, patented by Winslow Lewis in 1810. Its primary advantage was it used less than half the oil of prior oil lamps. It included a parabolic reflector behind the lamp and a magnifying lens made from four-inch-diameter green bottle glass was used in front of the lamp.

Lightroom: A glass enclosure at the top of the lighthouse tower, which housed the lighthouse optic, generally an electric light bulb.

Light station: A lighthouse complex, including a lighthouse tower, keepers' dwelling(s), fuel storage building, fog signal equipment building, and other necessary buildings.

Lighthouse: A light on top of a tower to provide an aid to navigation for mariners.

Lighthouse Board: A nine-member board appointed by the US Congress in 1852, established to manage lighthouses through-out the United States.

Litharge: Lead-based putty used to "seat" glass prisms to its brass frame such as in a Fresnel lens.

Logbook: A record book kept in a lighthouse and maintained daily by the keeper to record events as mandated by the US Lighthouse Establishment. Similar to a daily diary.

Luminous range: The range (distance) covered by a lighthouse increases with brightness of the light. See geographic range.

Magnetic deviation: Compass error due to close by metallic (ferrous) objects.

Magnetic north: The point at which the earth's north magnetic field converge near the true geographical North Pole. See variation.

Magnetic south: The point at which the earth's south magnetic field converge near the true geographical South Pole.

MHW (mean high water): The average of all the high water heights observed and recorded over many years. Used to reference the focal plane of a lighthouse or beacon.

Nautical mile: A unit of distance used primarily at sea. The average distance on the earth's latitude represented by one minute. A nautical mile equals approximately 1.1508 statute (land) miles.

Navigation: The science of accurately steering a vessel over water toward a planned destination.

Occultation: A light in which the total duration of light during each period is longer than the total duration of darkness and in which the intervals of darkness (occultation) are of equal periods. Occultation is created partially blocking (occulting), the light to make it appear flashing. Also called an eclipsing light. Opposite of flashing.

Offshore-type lighthouse: Light stations built offshore to replace lightships. Often called rock or stag lighthouses.

Order: The power rating of a Fresnel lens as determined by the radius distance of its internal light source to the lens. The greater the radius, the larger the lens; hence, the more prism rings required resulting in a brighter and wider outgoing light beam. Lens sizes and power range from first order (largest) to sixth order (smallest).

Parabolic reflector: See reflector.

Parapet: A lighthouse walkway with railings encircling a lighthouse lightroom. Often called a "catwalk."

Period: Time interval between "on and off" or "off and on" of light or sound cycles of the device characteristics.

Pharologist: One who studies or is interested in lighthouses. Derived from the world's first lighthouse built by Egyptians in Alexandria, Egypt, between 270 and 300 BC.

Pier: A structure extending into navigable waters for use as a landing place for vessels to protect or to form a harbor.

Prism: Triangular-shaped transparent glass or plastic concentric ring sections of a lighthouse Fresnel lens shaped and positioned to *refract* (bend) its light source to produce an outgoing horizontal light beam.

Radio beacon: Electronic equipment transmitting a coded signal used by mariners to locate the position of their vessels.

Red sector: A section of the lighthouse light that is colored or filtered red to warn mariners of dangerous obstacle ahead, such as shoals and rocks. Mariners must change course until the light is white again, thus avoiding the danger.

Reflection: Law of reflection suggests that angle of light striking a surface equals to the angle of light rebounding from that surface.

Reflector: A highly polished silver-plated bowl-shaped metallic parabolic device usually made of copper, placed behind a candle or oil lamp in a lightroom to reflect its light. Obsolete upon the invention of the Fresnel lens.

Refraction: Bending or slanting light waves as light passes between two medias, such as the prism of a lens and air.

Revolving light: A light made to revolve by clockworks to appear as having flashing characteristics.

Riprap: A loose arrangement of broken rocks or stone placed to help stem erosion.

Rock-type lighthouse: A lighthouse surrounded by the sea. (See off-shore tower.)

Sea level: The ocean's mean high water (MHW) as denoted on navigational charts.

Screw-pile-type lighthouse: Lighthouses built on poles that are "screwed" into the seabed floor. They often supported a small wooden building for the keeper with a light on top.

Shoal: A dangerous and shallow area in water, such as a sandbar or rock formation.

Skeletal-type lighthouse: Towers consisting of four or more strongly braced legs often enclosing keeper's quarters or workrooms and with a beacon on top. With their open design, they offer little resistance to the wind and waves and have withstood many storms. They are also used onshore, where the land cannot sustain the weight of a masonry tower.

Sound signal: See fog signal.

Sparkplug-type lighthouse: A caisson-type light tower that looks somewhat like a sparkplug used in a vehicle.

Stag-type lighthouse: A lighthouse not connected to a mainland, tended only by men. No families allowed.

Tender: A small vessel used to transport keeper, visitors, equipment, or food to isolated lighthouses.

Tower: A structure supporting the lantern of a lighthouse.

True north: The point at which longitude lines converge at the North Pole.

Variation: The angle between true north and magnetic north. Changes annually and currently ~20 degrees.

Ventilator: Round "ball" at the top of most lighthouse towers to exhaust heat from the lightroom, as well as from the oil lamp or light bulb, and for air circulation within the lightroom. Adjustable circular openings allow incoming air to be regulated to provide steady flow of air for the oil lamp light.

Watch room: A level of a lighthouse usually located immediately below the lightroom with storm-type porthole windows through which a lighthouse keeper may "watch" marine activity, weather, and water conditions during storm conditions, hence the name. Also, the room is where fuel and other supplies were kept and where the keeper prepared the lamp(s) for the night.

Wick hollow: A tubular hollow cotton wick designed to allow air to flow in and around thus allowing the fuel to burn more efficiently as well as smokeless and brighter than typical flat wicks.

Wickie: A nickname given to lighthouse keepers, derived from trimming the wicks of oil lamps.

Winslow Lewis: Former sea captain and lighthouse builder. Native of Wellfleet, Cape Cod, Massachusetts. The US government purchased the Winslow Lewis patent for a brighter lighting system and to modify all lighthouses in America with Lewis lamps. The oldest surviving lighthouse in America built by Winslow Lewis is Sapelo Island Light in Georgia.

ABOUT THE AUTHOR

BEN GREW UP in a Boston suburb of Newton, Massachusetts.

Lighthouses always fascinated him, especially those along the Massachusetts coastlines. How did they work? How can they be seen from so many miles, and what does an actual light look like up close?

Ben and his wife, Joanne, live on Cape Cod and are tour guides at Nobska Light. After sailing for many years, Ben's fascination toward lighthouses intensified whenever he and Joanne sailed close to Cape Cod's many lighthouses.

CPSIA information can be obtained
at www.ICGtesting.com
Printed in the USA
LVHW070430021021
699267LV00002B/3